OCT - - 2016

J959.7 WILLIS
Willis, Terri.
Vietnam /

P9-CJZ-902

WITHDRAWN

Vietnam

Vietnam

By Terri Willis

Enchantment of the World™
Second Series

Children's Press®
An Imprint of Scholastic Inc.
New York Toronto London Auckland Sydney
Mexico City New Delhi Hong Kong
Danbury, Connecticut

Alameda Free Library
1550 Oak Street
Alameda, CA 94501

Frontispiece: Rice terraces near Sapa

Consultant: Charles Keith, Department of History, Michigan State University, Lansing, Michigan

Please note: All statistics are as up-to-date as possible at the time of publication.

Book production by The Design Lab

Cataloging-in-Publication data is available from the Library of Congress
ISBN: 978-0-531-25605-3

No part of this publication may be reproduced in whole or in part, or stored in a retrieval system, or transmitted in any form or by any means, electronic, mechanical, photocopying, recording, or otherwise, without written permission of the publisher. For information regarding permission, write to Scholastic Inc., 557 Broadway, New York, NY 10012.

© 2013 by Scholastic Inc.
All rights reserved. Published in 2013 by Children's Press, an imprint of Scholastic Inc.
Printed in the United States of America 141
SCHOLASTIC, CHILDREN'S PRESS, and associated logos are trademarks and/or registered trademarks of Scholastic Inc.

1 2 3 4 5 6 7 8 9 10 R 22 21 20 19 18 17 16 15 14 13

Vietnam

Contents

Cover photo:
Boats in the Mekong Delta

Central coast

Gibbons

CHAPTER ONE

Family Focus

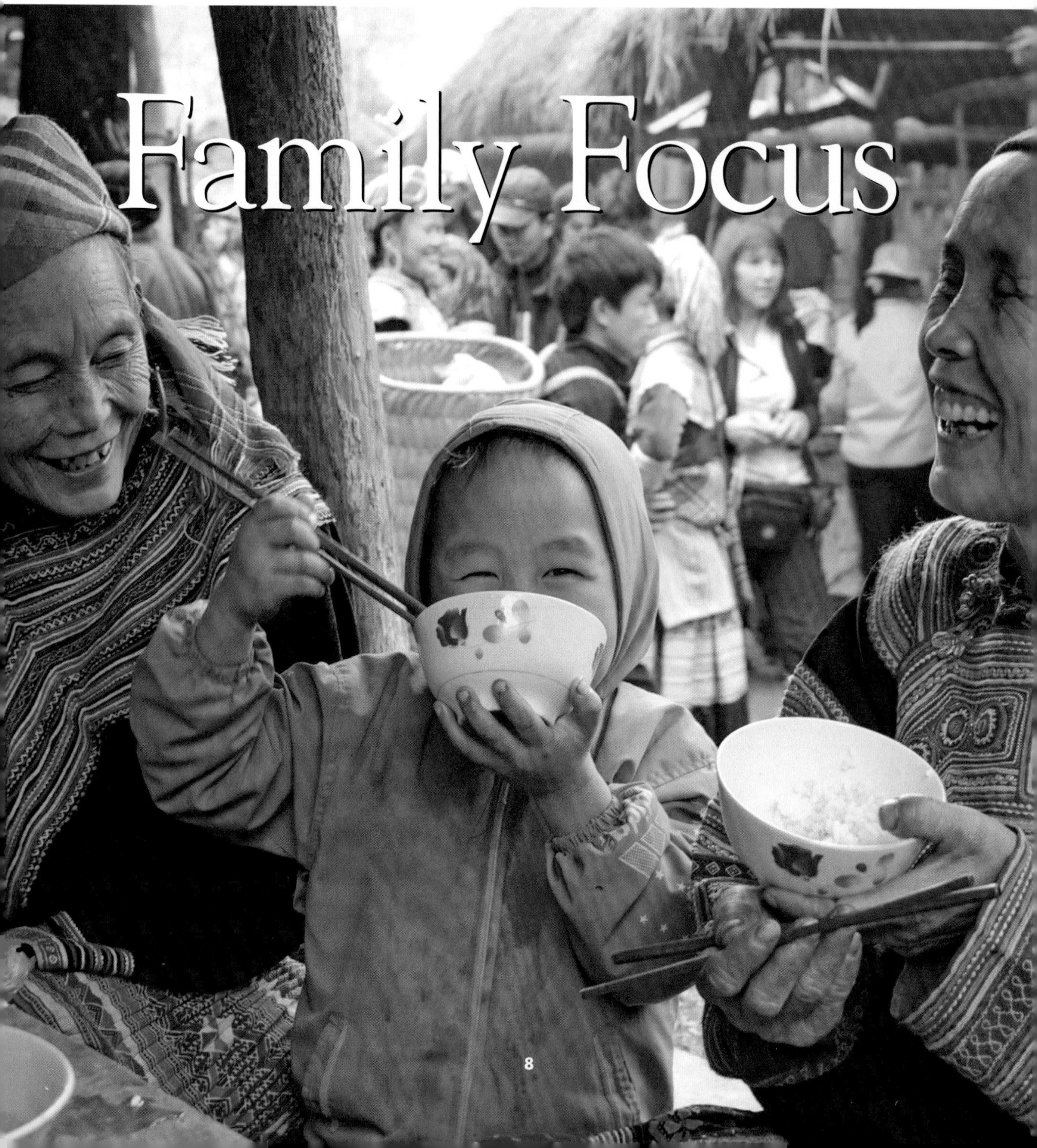

FAMILY HOLDS THE HIGHEST IMPORTANCE IN VIETNAMESE society. This is the key to understanding the Vietnamese people and their culture.

Opposite: **A family from the Hmong ethnic group shares a laugh while eating lunch.**

Respect for elders is part of the country's tradition. The oldest son in a family has more authority than his siblings, and grandparents receive great respect. Young people obey their parents' wishes. They care for them until death. Vietnamese people also worship relatives who have passed on.

In many ways, the family is more significant than the individuals within it. Family members typically behave in ways that serve the family as a whole, rather than the individual relatives. Having a good family name that is respected in the community is very important.

Vietnamese people feel a constant connection with their relatives. A Vietnamese monk, Thich Nhat Hanh, once wrote, "If you look deeply into the palm of your hand, you will see your parents and all generations of your ancestors. All of them are alive in this moment. Each is present in your body. You are the continuation of each of these people."

Vietnam
CHINA
Dong Van Karst Plateau Geopark
Cao Bang
Ba Be Natl. Park
Lai Chau
Fan Si Pan
Black R.
Red R.
Dien Bien Phu
Thai Nguyen
Son La
Son Tay
Hanoi
Ba Vi
Hong Gai
Haiphong
Thai Binh
Cat Ba Natl. Park
Cuc Phuong
Nam Dinh
Ma R.
Nightingale I.
LAOS
Thanh Hoa
Ca R.
Gulf of Tonkin
Hainan
South China Sea
Vu Quang Natl. Park
Mui Ron
Mekong R.
THAILAND
Phong Nha-Ke Bang National Park
Quang Tri
Hue
Da Nang
Bach Ma Natl. Park
Cai R.
Paracel Islands
VIETNAM
Cities of over 200,000 people
Other cities
National capital
0
200 miles
0
300 kilometers
Tay Son
Qui Nhon
Ba R.
Tonle Sap
Mekong R.
Yok Don Natl. Park
Nha Trang
CAMBODIA
Da Lat
Cam Ranh
Phan Rang
Mui Dinh
Cat Tien Natl. Park
Tay Ninh
N
W
E
S
Gulf of Thailand
Mekong R.
Ho Chi Minh City (Saigon)
Vung Tau
Phan Thiet
Cu Lao
Phu Quoc (disputed)
Rach Gia
Can Tho
Pte. de Ca Mau
Con Son
Con Dao Natl. Park
Spratly Islands

A Vietnamese family goes for a spin in Chau Doc, in southern Vietnam. The average family in Vietnam has two children.

These tight family bonds are at the heart of how Vietnam functions as a nation and as a society. In Vietnam today, large numbers of people live on relatively small parcels of land. They get along in these crowded conditions because they are used to living closely with family members.

The Vietnamese people have endured much throughout history. They have had to fight for their freedom from invading nations. There have been civil wars as well, most recently during the Vietnam War, which lasted for two decades, ending in 1975. They have endured great poverty, too. But in recent years, Vietnam's rising economy is helping many people find a better life. Through all of this, Vietnamese families have stayed together and stayed strong.

CHAPTER

TWO

As a River Flows

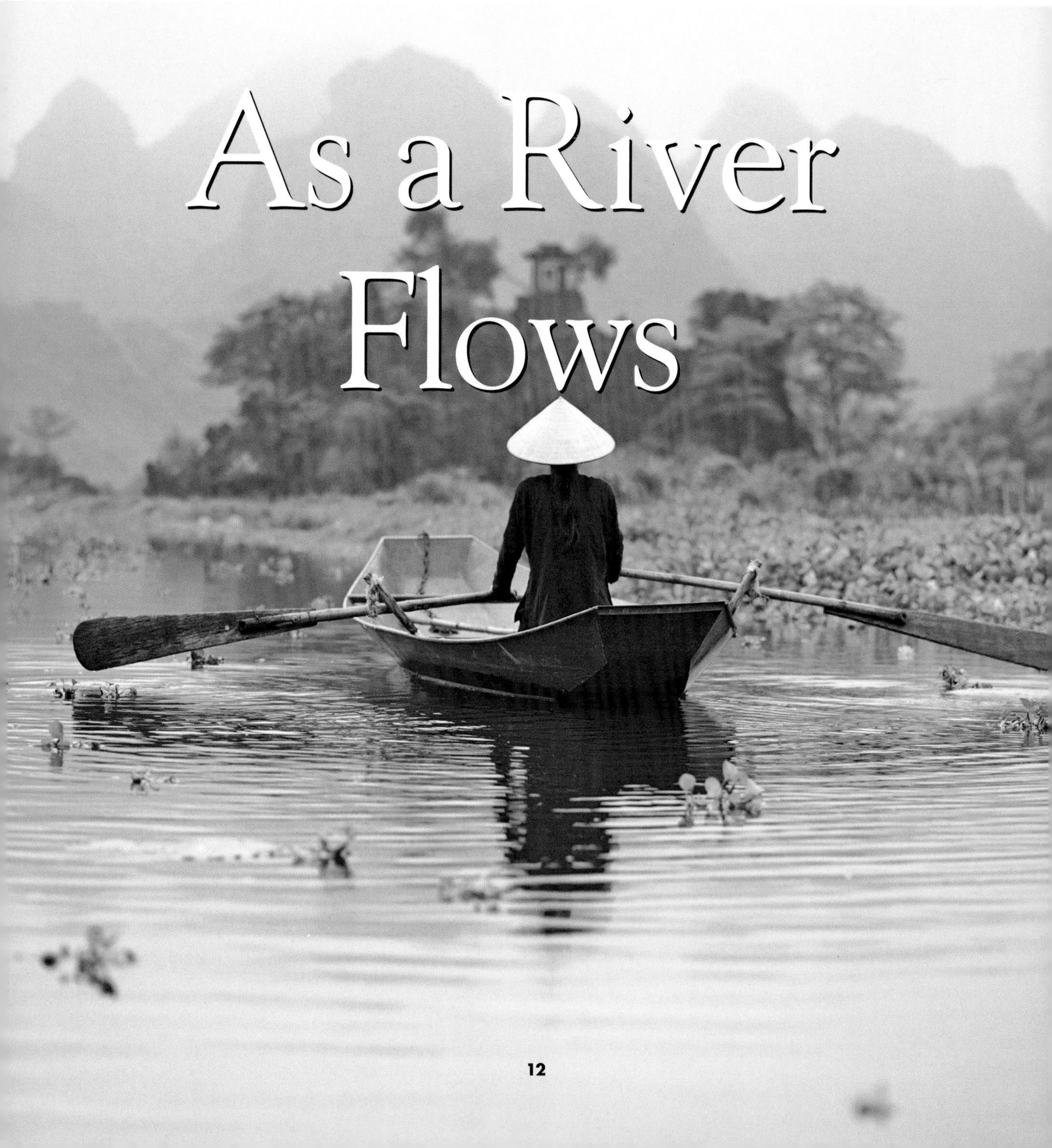

Like a flowing river, the country of Vietnam gracefully arches, widens, and narrows, as it forms the eastern edge of the Indochinese Peninsula in Southeast Asia. The country consists of two broad river deltas, at its northern and southern tips, connected by a long, slender, curving stretch of mountain and coast. North to south, Vietnam is 1,023 miles (1,646 kilometers) long. At its narrowest point, it measures only 31 miles (50 km) east to west.

Opposite: **A woman rows up the Perfume River in central Vietnam. The river's name comes from the fragrance of the many orchids that fall into the river in the autumn.**

China lies to the north of Vietnam, and Laos and Cambodia to the west. In the east, the country is bordered by the Gulf of Tonkin and the South China Sea. Vietnam's territory also includes thousands of islands.

Vietnam is a relatively small country, only a bit larger than the U.S. state of New Mexico. It has three geographical regions. From north to south they are Bac Bo, Trung Bo, and Nam Bo.

Vietnam's Geographical Features

Area: 127,882 square miles (331,212 sq km)

Highest Elevation: Fan Si Pan, 10,312 feet (3,143 m) above sea level

Lowest Elevation: Sea level, along the coast

Greatest Distance North to South: 1,023 miles (1,646 km)

Greatest Distance East to West: 372 miles (600 km)

Longest River: Mekong, 2,597 miles (4,180 km) long

Average High Temperature: Ho Chi Minh City: 89°F (32°C) in January; 90°F (32°C) in July. Hanoi: 67°F (19°C) in January; 92°F (33°C) in July

Average Low Temperature: Ho Chi Minh City: 70°F (21°C) in January; 76°F (24°C) in July. Hanoi: 57°F (14°C) in January; 79°F (26°C) in July

Average Annual Precipitation: 78 inches (198 cm) in the Mekong Delta; 66 inches (168 cm) in the Red River delta

Nearly three-quarters of Vietnam is mountainous.

Bac Bo

Bac Bo is the northern region of Vietnam. The Hoang Lien Son Mountains rise in its northern reaches, forming the border with China. These towering mountains are an eastern extension of the Himalayas. They include the nation's tallest peak, Fan Si Pan, which rises 10,312 feet (3,143 meters). In these mountains, waterfalls plunge down the steep cliffs. Caves are abundant. The valleys are green with thick jungles.

Farther south, valleys and plateaus stretch to the Red River delta. The Red River begins in China and flows 714 miles (1,149 km) to the Gulf of Tonkin. As the river approaches Vietnam's coastal lowlands, it fans out, depositing silt to create a muddy and fertile region. The river deposits so much silt at its mouth that the delta advances another 300 feet (90 m) into the gulf each year.

The silt deposits are rich in nutrients, making the soil good for farming. Rice has been harvested in the Red River delta for thousands of years. The Vietnamese people have built many canals, dikes, and irrigation systems to channel the waters of the Red River to the fields where it is needed. During heavy rains, the river proves it cannot be tamed. Damaging floodwaters sometimes overflow its banks.

Boats carry rice plants along a canal in the Red River delta. More than 1,600 varieties of rice are grown in the country.

Much of the land in north-central Vietnam is made of karst limestone. Water can easily erode this kind of rock, creating caves. The Phong Nha-Ke Bang National Park includes three hundred caves and the longest underground river in the world.

Trung Bo

Trung Bo is the middle region of Vietnam. It is a slender strip of land that stretches from the South China Sea in the east to the Truong Son Mountains in the west. More than two hundred rivers have cut deep valleys through the mountains as they flow toward the sea.

In the center of the narrow region are high plateaus. Some of this is good farmland with rich, red soil. Tea, coffee, and rubber are the main crops here. In many other areas, however, the soil is poor and is not good for agriculture, so many people make their living from fishing. Many small ethnic communities are tucked away in the plateau region. Nearer the coast, beautiful beaches, dunes, and lagoons dot the landscape.

Peaceful, sandy bays line the central coast of Vietnam.

Up the Mountain

One of the world's longest and highest nonstop cable cars belongs to the Ba Na Cable Car Service near the city of Da Nang. The cable car stretches 16,542 feet (5,042 m) from the foot of Ba Na Mountain to the peak of neighboring Vong Nguyet Mountain. The ride takes fifteen minutes. Before it was built, traveling steep mountain passes was the only way to reach the top of the mountain and enjoy the stunning views.

The Marble Mountains lie near the middle of the region. They are formed of karst and are filled with caves. Near the top of these five peaks are dozens of caves that contain statues of the Buddha.

Nam Bo

In the south of Vietnam is the Nam Bo region. The Mekong River is the major geographic feature in this part of the country. The river flows for 2,597 miles (4,180 km) from its headwaters in Tibet, through Myanmar (Burma), Laos, Thailand, Cambodia, and Vietnam, to its mouth at the South China Sea. The Mekong's silt deposits have created much of the land in this region, and continue to build more land. Each year the deposits extend about 250 feet (75 m) farther into the sea.

The water and nutrients provided by the Mekong make the Nam Bo the country's largest rice-producing region. Fishing, especially for shrimp, is also a major industry, and the area is full of shrimp farms.

Looking at Vietnam's Cities

Ho Chi Minh City (right), formerly known as Saigon, is Vietnam's largest city by far. Its population was 7,396,446 in 2009. The city is growing quickly because a steady stream of people from rural areas is moving there in search of better lives. As the country's commercial and industrial center, Ho Chi Minh City is crowded, noisy, and fast-paced. Visitors there find plenty to do, from shopping to eating in modern restaurants to touring interesting temples and museums, which highlight the city's historical significance.

Vietnam's second-largest city is its capital, Hanoi, which has a population of 6,472,200. Haiphong is the nation's third-largest city, home to about 1,907,705 people. Located in the north of the country, it contains Vietnam's main seaport. Nearby Ha Long Bay is considered a gem by the Vietnamese and visitors alike. In the bay, craggy karst rock towers rise hundreds of feet above the water. Many consider it to be one of the world's most beautiful natural wonders.

The city of Da Nang, in central Vietnam, has a population of 887,069 people. It is a growing industrial area with a busy port and lovely bay. The city is home to the Museum of Cham Sculpture, which holds artifacts from the ancient Champa kingdom that once ruled central Vietnam. On view are several hundred sandstone, bronze, and terra-cotta monuments collected from Cham temples surrounding the countryside.

Hue was the imperial capital of Vietnam until 1945, when Hanoi became the capital. Today, the city has 340,000 residents. They live amid memories of that glorious past, although much of the ancient city was destroyed during the Vietnam War. The beautiful Perfume River winds through the city of Hue. On its north bank are the Forbidden Purple City, home for 150 years to the kings of the Nguyen dynasty; and the grand Imperial City, which has beautiful palaces, gardens, temples, and ponds. Both are found within the tall walls of the Hue Citadel. The city's tallest landmark, the seven-story Thien Mu Pagoda (left), is just upstream.

On the Mekong: Dams and Damage

The Mekong River is at the center of life in the Nam Bo region. It is used for travel, fishing, and growing rice. But a more modern use of the river—as a source of hydroelectric power—threatens all the other ways the river is used.

China has built four large dams on the Mekong and plans to build four more. Other nations along the river are also planning to build dams. These dams and the reservoirs they create regulate the flow of water in order to generate electricity in hydroelectric plants. The dams make it possible to hold back water during the rainy season, so the river does not flood. Then, during a drought, water can be released to keep the river flowing and the hydroelectric plants operating.

Unfortunately, these dams can be a problem for Vietnam, because the country depends on the changes in the river's flow for food production. During the dry season, farmers grow crops in the rich soil of the riverbeds. When the waters are heavier, they flood the fields, helping rice grow. The dams limit the flow of sediment down the river, which damages rice production.

Changes to the Mekong also hurt Vietnam's fishing industry and could threaten many animal species. More than 1,200 species of fish live in the Mekong—only the Amazon River in South America has greater biodiversity—but many of these could face serious challenges. The dams block the path of migrating fish. Fish from the Mekong are an important part of the diets of millions of people living in the delta. One species in particular danger is not a fish, but a mammal. The Irrawaddy freshwater dolphin is sometimes considered "the soul of the Mekong." These dolphins are extremely rare, and their numbers are decreasing. New dams upriver will accelerate their decline.

An agreement among all the countries along the Mekong is necessary. China is by far the most powerful of these countries, and it is not likely to change its plans to build more dams. It stands to gain much from the electricity, and the dams are not considered so damaging to the environment in China. In fact, Chinese officials point out that the dams are actually helping the environment. They say that it is better for China to get its much-needed energy through a clean and renewable energy source, such as hydroelectricity, than by burning coal, which releases harmful pollutants into the air. It will be difficult to find a solution to this problem that will be good for Vietnam as well as its neighbors upstream.

Islands

Vietnam lays claim to thousands of islands off its coast. They range from small, rocky peaks rising above the waves to large landmasses that are home to many people.

Vietnam's largest island group, the Ha Long Bay archipelago, includes 1,969 islands. Most are formed from limestone karst. The karst has eroded into large tower shapes, giving the islands a distinctive appearance. One of them, Cat Ba Island, is an important nature reserve, home to some rare species, including a monkey called the Cat Ba langur, which lives only on that island. This area's beauty attracts more than two million visitors each year.

Ha Long Bay is part of the Gulf of Tonkin, in northern Vietnam.

The Spratlys include about 750 small islands. About 45 of them are occupied by military forces.

Some of the islands claimed by Vietnam are also claimed by other nations. Both Vietnam and China claim the Spratly Islands, the largest archipelago in the South China Sea. Other nations also laying claim to these islands are Brunei, Malaysia, the Philippines, and Taiwan. The Spratly Islands have attracted the attention of so many countries because they are rich in oil and natural gas, have abundant fishing opportunities, and have great biological diversity. International efforts to resolve the dispute have failed. In the meantime, various countries have established military bases and small communities on the islands to aid their ownership claims. The conflicting claims have prevented conservation measures from being put into place in the islands. Current problems include pollution, the destruction of animal habitats, and overfishing.

Wet and Dry

Vietnam's climate is dominated by monsoons, or winds, that change the seasons. In summer, from May to October, the air over the land warms more quickly than the air over the waters of the Indian and Pacific Oceans. This warm air rises, and the cooler ocean air blows in over the land, carrying plenty of moisture. The moisture falls as rain, causing the wet monsoon season. The monsoons of summer bring an average of 72 inches (183 centimeters) of rain to the nation. The heaviest rains fall in the central highlands. This area receives an average of 130 inches (330 cm) of rain during the wet season. In winter, from November

Monsoon season brings heavy rains and frequent flooding.

to April, the air over the land is cooler than the air over the sea. Dry winds blow southward, beginning over the land and moving toward the warmer oceans, keeping clouds away.

Northern Vietnam is cooler than other parts of the country. In the mountains near the Chinese border, the temperature often dips below 40 degrees Fahrenheit (4 degrees Celsius) in the winter. In Hanoi, in the lowlands of the north, the average high in January is 67°F (19°C); and in July, the warmest month, temperatures reach an average high of 92°F (33°C).

Hot soup wards off the winter chill in northern Vietnam.

A tropical storm hit Da Nang in 2006, littering the street with trees.

It gets even warmer farther south, with highs of 95°F (35°C) or hotter during the summer. Southern cities do not cool off very much in the winter. Ho Chi Minh City has an average daily high temperature of 89°F (32°C) in January, its coolest month.

Typhoons, which are severe tropical hurricanes, are sometimes a problem in central Vietnam. The tremendous force of the winds and waves can do severe damage to the coastline and beaches. Boats, homes, businesses, and wildlife are destroyed.

CHAPTER THREE

Bursting with Life

Vietnam has extraordinary diversity in its plants and animals. More than 840 bird species fly over Vietnam, and nearly 3,200 types of fish swim in its waters. The country is home to some 310 species of mammals, 260 kinds of reptiles, and 160 types of amphibians. These animals live amid the many thousands of types of plants that grow there. The number of identified species is constantly increasing as biologists scour the country. In 2010 alone, 59 new species were discovered. These include a wildly colored gecko, a moray eel, and six kinds of bamboo.

Opposite: **The red-shanked douc is an endangered monkey that lives only in Vietnam and Laos. Doucs spend most of their time in the trees and can leap 20 feet (6 m) from one branch to another.**

Sadly, many species in Vietnam are in danger of disappearing. Delacour's langur, which lives only in northern Vietnam, is one of the world's most endangered primates. Fewer than 250 of these leaf-eating monkeys remain in the wild. In 2011, the Javan rhinoceros was declared extinct in Vietnam. It once lived throughout much of Southeast Asia, but now only about forty of these rhinos survive on the island nation of Indonesia.

Bamboo is a giant, fast-growing member of the grass family. In Vietnam, it sometimes grows 12 inches (30 cm) a day.

Plants

More than thirteen thousand types of plants have been identified in Vietnam. Many of them have uses in medicine, in construction, and as food for people or animals. Rice is Vietnam's main crop. Other important crops include bananas, pineapple, coconut, and bamboo. All of these grow wild in Vietnam but are now cultivated by farmers.

The kind of plants found in different parts of Vietnam depends, in part, on elevation. Hardwood trees such as mahogany, teak, oak, and ebony grow in mountainous areas. These are prized for making furniture, but in recent years so many of these trees have been cut down that some hillsides are bare. At lower mountain elevations, pines and other evergreens are plentiful. Bamboo thickets grow in the mountains as well.

Vines, such as rattan and liana, are common in the forests of Vietnam. They are so thick it is sometimes hard for people to make their way through the forests. Near the coast, palms and fruit trees grow, and mangroves and sea grasses line the water's edge.

Flowers and flowering shrubs such as rhododendrons and camellias add color to the landscape, especially in Vietnam's warmer regions. Delicate orchids grow naturally in Vietnam, and many are harvested and shipped around the world. Flowering epiphytes grow high in trees. These plants depend on trees for support, growing up to the top branches where they can find the rainwater and sunlight they need to survive. They do not put roots into the ground. Instead, they collect moisture from the humid air or the dampness of the tree bark.

Saving the Mangroves

Mangrove trees thrive in the saltwater that would kill most plants. Their roots rise from the seabed and look like fingers above the water's surface. Below the surface, the tangle of roots provides shelter for baby fish and other sea creatures. Mangrove forests protect coastal communities during storms, blocking the wind and waves that could damage homes. They also hold the sand and soil in place, preventing erosion.

In recent decades, many mangrove forests in Vietnam and elsewhere around the world have been cut down. Some have been cut for timber, while others have been replaced with houses and golf courses. Many are cleared to make way for shrimp farms. Raising shrimp is a huge industry in Vietnam, and one that often provides poor people with a living. However, a growing number of people in Vietnam are trying to protect the mangroves and are encouraging farming techniques that don't threaten these forests.

The National Flower

The pink lotus was officially named the national flower of Vietnam in 2012. This came at the end of a two-year contest in which people voted for the flower that best represented their country. Other contenders included water lilies, yellow apricot, bamboo, rice flowers, peach blossoms, arecas (a type of palm), and tree orchids. The lotus won about 70 percent of the vote.

Lotus plants grow in ponds or rivers. The flower, which has many petals, reaches up above the water. The lotus is a symbol of purity, beauty, majesty, grace, and wealth. In some Asian religions, it is also a symbol of perfection because it emerges from the dirty muck of a pool and blooms into beauty.

Residents of Vietnam's crowded cities make room for beautiful plants. People have planted many tamarind trees in Ho Chi Minh City, for example. The city is filled with splashes of yellow and red when the trees are in bloom. Purple and red bougainvillaeas add color to many cities as well.

Animals

Vietnam is home to some very large mammals, including elephants, wild oxen, and bears. Small mammals such as mice also live in Vietnam, among other kinds of creatures of all sizes.

Wild pigs, otters, jackals, mongooses, tigers, leopards, tapirs, porcupines, and hares are all found in Vietnam. Many kinds of monkeys live in Vietnam as well, including rhesus monkeys, macaques, and gibbons. Common domesticated animals include water buffalo, cattle, pigs, goats, ducks, chicken, cats, and dogs.

Water buffalo are huge, mild-mannered creatures. Vietnamese farmers use them to pull plows, lumber, and other goods.

The waters of Vietnam are filled with fish and other creatures. Fishing is a major industry in the country. Important species include carp, catfish, tuna, mackerel, and tilapia. Lobster, shrimp, and crab are also sold there. Reptiles in Vietnam include crocodiles as well as cobras, pythons, and other snakes. A wide variety of lizards live in the country, such as geckos, monitors, and flying lizards.

Most of Vietnam's 770 bird species are found in the Mekong Delta region and along the coasts. They include water-loving birds such as storks, cranes, herons, egrets, ducks, and cormorants. Other birds found in Vietnam include hornbills, laughing thrushes, and brown hawk owls.

The Cat Tien Bear Rescue Center

The Bear Rescue Center in Vietnam's Cat Tien National Park provides a safe place for bears that have been mistreated in captivity. Most bears there have been removed from run-down zoos or other ailing facilities, and many have a fear of humans. Workers at the rescue center treat the animals in a calm, caring way. They feed them and treat their injuries until the bears get stronger. The workers then teach the bears to live on their own in the wilderness. Meat is hidden in the forest so the animals recover their natural instinct for looking for food. Finding a safe place to return the bears to the wild is difficult for rescue center officials. Bears are hunted so heavily in Vietnam that releasing the animals into their natural habitat often means releasing them to their deaths.

Environmental Problems and Solutions

Vietnam's environment suffered great damage during the war with the United States. Heavy bombing by the United States destroyed landscapes. U.S. forces also sprayed chemicals on trees to strip them of leaves, so soldiers could see people moving through the forest from airplanes above. This destroyed some 5 million acres (2 million hectares) of forest. Half the nation's coastal mangroves were wiped out. Large areas of the country, once lush, became barren.

American soldiers sit in a devastated forest during the Vietnam War. It is estimated that the U.S. military destroyed more than 40 percent of Vietnam's forests during the war.

Much of Cat Ba Island in Ha Long Bay is covered in thick forest.

But it is nature's way to rebound. In Vietnam, that has slowly begun to happen in recent decades. In some places, the forest is recovering on its own, and in some places, humans are helping. The government has begun replanting forests and mangrove swamps and is trying to stop harmful practices such as clear-cutting forests for lumber. It has also established national parks to help preserve natural areas that remain. Its goal is to restore much of Vietnam's wilderness to the lush green land that it was before the war.

Another cause of environmental decline in Vietnam is the poverty of so many of its people. Though illegal logging may carry a hefty punishment, it can also bring in money for

The population of gibbons in Vietnam has dropped dramatically, because they are being hunted and because their habitat is being destroyed.

poor villagers struggling to feed their families. The same goes for poaching, or killing, endangered animals. Some animals are very valuable because people are willing to pay a lot for their furs or other body parts. For many poor Vietnamese, the potential reward is worth risking the possible penalty.

Vietnam has established thirty national parks and hundreds of natural reserve areas to help protect the environment. Cuc Phuong, Vietnam's oldest national park, was established in 1962 in the Red River delta of northern Vietnam. The park protects leopards, gibbons, macaques, and many other animals. Vietnam's largest wildlife preserve is Yok Don National Park, which covers nearly 300,000 acres (120,000 ha) of lush forest and mountains along the Cambodian border. Tigers, leopards, sambar deer, and wild elephants are among this park's many endangered species.

In 2010, Vietnam became part of the Global Geoparks Network, a program that works to conserve areas that are important geologically. Vietnam's first such park, the Dong Van Karst Plateau Geopark, is located along the border with China. It is a preserve of ancient fossils, many four hundred to six hundred million years old, which are embedded in the limestone in the park.

Tigers were once widespread in Southeast Asia, but it is estimated that only about twenty wild tigers live in Vietnam today. They survive in remote mountain forests.

CHAPTER FOUR

Becoming Vietnam

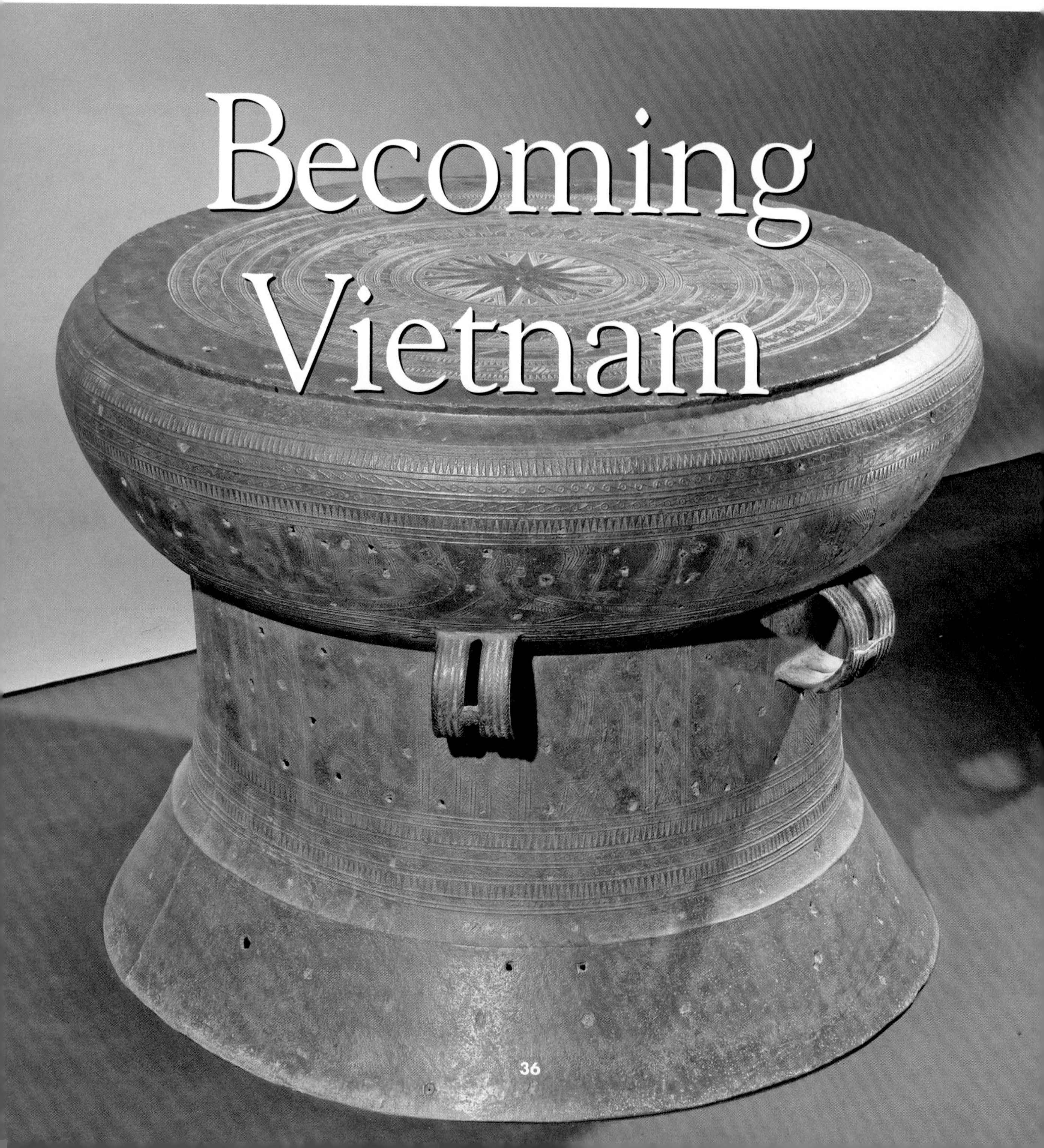

ACCORDING TO LEGEND, MANY CENTURIES AGO the Dragon Lord of the Sea, Lac Long Quan, married a beautiful mountain fairy, Au Co. Together, they gave life to one hundred sons. When both parents yearned for their childhood homes, they divided their sons between them. The mother returned to the mountains, taking fifty sons with her, while the father returned to the sea with their other fifty sons. These one hundred children formed the beginnings of the Vietnamese people. Some lived in the mountains, and others near the sea, just as the Vietnamese still do today. The eldest son, Hung Vuong, became the first emperor of the Hung dynasty, ruling over much of what is now northern Vietnam. He was succeeded by Hung Vuong II, who in turn was followed by Hung Vuong III. This continued through eighteen different Hung Vuongs. The Hung dynasty reigned until 258 BCE.

Opposite: **The Dong Son people of the Red River delta began making bronze drums more than two thousand years ago.**

This legend has been passed down through generations of Vietnamese families. It is a way to explain things that are not known for certain. The story of the Hung dynasty weaves

The Dong Son people grew rice in the Red River delta. They also traded with other people throughout Southeast Asia.

together threads of truth and shreds of fantasy. They are part of Vietnam's prehistory, the time before history was written down and preserved.

Early Migrants

Many of today's Vietnamese people descended from early inhabitants of the Ma River valley in northern Vietnam. They migrated from southern China and eastern Southeast Asia into this region about three hundred thousand years ago. During this time, humans were just learning to use rough stone tools. In cliff dwellings in Thanh Hoa Province of northern Vietnam, archaeologists have discovered rugged tools made of basalt. These tools date back about fifty thousand years.

Much later, around 100 BCE, another group in northern Vietnam was making axes of stone with polished edges. These were the Dong Son people, who are often considered the first true Vietnamese. Eventually they became known as Lac Viet, the "people of the valley." They inhabited nearly the entire Red River delta. They left behind many remnants of their culture, most notably bronze drums found throughout the region. The Viet, as they came to be called, spread down the coast. This journey, known as Nam Tien, or the "March to the South," took centuries. As the Vietnamese moved south, they came into contact with many other cultures and peoples. Often this contact was peaceful, but sometimes wars broke out as the various groups learned to live alongside one another.

The early Vietnamese were skilled potters. This jug is from the first to third century CE.

Chinese Rule

The Chinese conquered the land of the Viet in 111 BCE. They brought better tools such as metal plows and taught the Viet how to improve their irrigation system. The Chinese began silk production, opened schools, and taught writing. The Viet adopted the philosophy of Confucianism, which guided Chinese life, and absorbed much of Chinese culture.

During hundreds of years of Chinese rule, the Viet yearned for their independence. They maintained their own language and tried to expel the Chinese. Their first success at gaining some independence came under the leadership of a fearless woman named Trung Trac. After the Chinese killed her hus-

Confucius was a deeply influential Chinese teacher and philosopher. He lived from 551 to 479 BCE.

band, she led a rebellion in 40 CE that knocked them from power. She became queen and ruled the Viet with the help of her sister, Trung Nhi. Their reign lasted less than three years before some twenty thousand Chinese troops stormed in to retake the area. Though the Trung sisters did not achieve lasting independence for the Viet, they provided hope that such freedom was possible. It would be another nine hundred years, though, before that dream was realized. In 938, a Vietnamese rebellion led by Ngo Quyen rid the region of the Chinese invaders. At this time, the area was known as Nam Viet.

Many Cham sculptures depict figures from Hinduism, such as the god Shiva.

The Trung Sisters

Nearly every city and town in Vietnam has a Hai Ba Trung Street, named after the Trung sisters, who bravely led a rebellion against the Chinese and reestablished Viet rule. Even after the Chinese returned, the Trung sisters remained heroes to the Viet. They gave hope and inspiration to generations of Viet people who, like them, would also have to fight off invasion by the Chinese.

Ngo Quyen: National Hero

For centuries, the Vietnamese people struggled to defeat the Chinese who controlled their land. No one was successful, though, until Ngo Quyen, in about 938. He devised a brilliant plan. At low tide, he and his troops planted a sturdy barrier of iron-tipped stakes into the bed of the Bach Dang River. Then, when the tide came in and the water rose, he lured the Chinese fleet up the river. The boats sailed right over the stakes without realizing they were there. When the Chinese realized it was a trap, they tried to retreat down the river into the sea. But by then the tide was low and the boats were impaled on the stakes. The entire fleet sank, and Ngo Quyen and his troops claimed victory. Ngo Quyen remains a national hero in Vietnam. Monuments to his bravery are common throughout the country.

Indian Settlements

During the time that China controlled the northern part of what is now Vietnam, Indian culture was greatly influencing the southern part. In the first century CE, sailors from India established ports along the southern coast. Many of these ports became small kingdoms, and Hinduism, a religion that began in India, spread throughout the region. Champa was the most prominent of these small kingdoms. By the tenth century, it was an important stop on the trade routes that stretched from western Asia to southern China.

The Le and Tran Dynasties

After Ngo Quyen succeeded in forcing the Chinese out of the region, he became the leader of the Vietnamese territory. He died

The Ruins of My Son

One of the most magnificent sites in Vietnam was abandoned and forgotten for generations. Cham rulers established the My Son complex of brick temples in the fourth century near their capital of Simhapura, present-day Tra Kieu, in central Vietnam. Cham kings were buried there. Beginning in the seventh century, each Cham dynasty and king added temples, until there were more than seventy intricately detailed buildings. The Cham believed My Son was the land of gods, so only Hindu priests, their servants, and their dancers were allowed to live on the grounds. My Son remained in use until the fourteenth century, when a Cham king gave up the land in exchange for a Vietnamese princess's hand in marriage. After that, My Son was deserted, until the French came upon the site in 1898.

In the years that followed, archaeologists carefully cataloged all of the site's artifacts. Most sculptures were relocated to museums in Vietnam. The temples were well preserved, because the Chams had excellent masonry skills.

During the Vietnam War, some Vietnamese forces made My Son a base of operations, and American troops bombed much of it into rubble. The largest and most intricate tower, which stood 79 feet (24 m) tall, was destroyed. But about twenty temples remain intact.

Each temple has distinct features. Many have artwork carved directly into the brick. One displays an ancient god standing on a lotus flower balanced on an elephant head. Another depicts two elephants with their trunks wrapped around a coconut tree. Carved lion faces with fanged teeth stare out from the side of one temple, and horned gargoyles protect the entry at another. Visitors to the site see large craters and piles of rubble, reminders of the majesty that once existed and the bombs that brought it down.

only five years later, however. For the next twenty-five years, a dozen local warlords fought for control. Finally, in 968, Dinh Bo Linh became the ruler. He ensured some safety for Vietnam by paying money to China in return for a promise that it would not invade the country. These payments continued until the 1800s.

Ly Thai To (right) moved the capital from Hoa Lu to what is now Hanoi because the area around Hanoi has many rivers and lakes, which help with transportation and trade.

More stability was provided in 1009 when Ly Thai To came to power, beginning the Ly dynasty. He and his successors ruled Vietnam for more than two hundred years. Thang Long, a city in northern Vietnam, became the capital. Eventually, this city became known as Hanoi, and it still serves as Vietnam's capital today. Under the Ly dynasty, Vietnam's economy improved. Better irrigation helped provide water to grow more rice. More people became landowners. The first university was established in the capital in 1076. The military grew stronger.

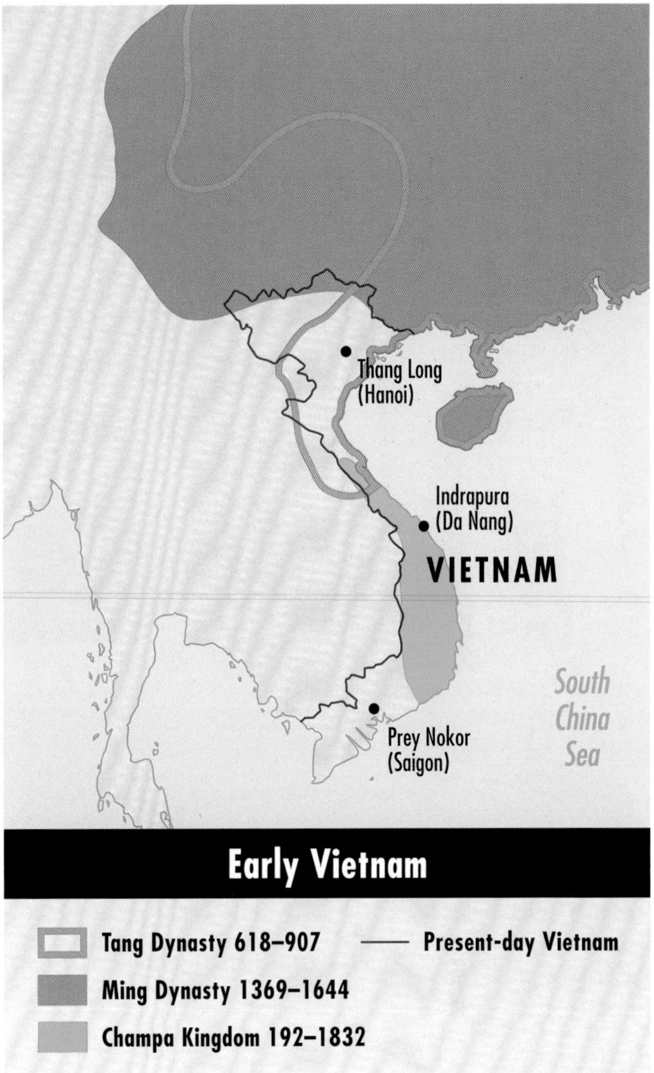

Early Vietnam

In 1225, the Tran dynasty gained control of the country. Under the Tran rulers, the military grew even stronger. In 1287, the general Tran Hung Dao was able to hold back the powerful Mongolian army, which by then ruled China. He used the same technique Ngo Quyen had used against the Chinese some three hundred years earlier: he planted metal stakes in a riverbed. More than four hundred Mongol ships were captured or destroyed.

Although the military was successful, it drew resources away from the rest of the economy. When a severe famine hit northern Vietnam in the late 1300s, hungry peasants revolted,

Vietnam's first university was established in 1076 at the Temple of Literature in Hanoi.

and the Tran rulers were overthrown. The country's instability made it possible for Chinese troops to once again take control.

The Chinese Return

This time the Chinese were harsh rulers. They destroyed works of art and accounts of history. They forced peasants to mine for precious gold and hunted their forests for valuable elephant tusks and rhinoceros horns. The Chinese hoped that by getting rid of the things that united the Vietnamese people, they could more easily control them. But instead, the Vietnamese became more determined to resist. A landowner named Le Loi led a band of soldiers through ten years of fighting before they defeated the Chinese in 1427.

The Le Dynasty

Le Loi became King Le Thai To, the founder of the Le dynasty. His son, Le Thanh Tong, became the dynasty's greatest king. During his rule, from 1460 to 1497, women won some civil rights. Math and science boomed. He led the country in new agricultural practices that increased grain production. Vietnam added more land to the south, and became a major military force in the mainland of Southeast Asia. This period is considered Vietnam's golden age.

It did not last long, however. By the sixteenth century, two powerful and warring clans had divided Vietnam: the Trinh in the north, and the Nguyen in the south. Though the Le dynasty still ruled, it had no real power.

Under Le Thanh Tong (left), the Le dynasty established a new legal code and conquered the kingdom of Champa.

This instability made it easy for Europeans to gain a foothold in Vietnam. Dutch, French, and Portuguese all established trading bases and partnerships. Missionaries also came to the region and converted thousands of Vietnamese people to Christianity.

The Tay Son Rebellion

During this period, there was much poverty. As the peasants' hunger grew, so did their anger. For decades, Vietnamese rulers had pushed back against small rebellions. But in 1788 a larger and more successful rebellion had gained control of much of the region.

Three brothers from the village of Tay Son on Vietnam's south-central coast led the Tay Son Rebellion. The brothers

The Nguyen dynasty built its capital in Hue. Large urns sit in front of a temple at the Nguyen palace.

pledged to take the property of wealthy landowners and give it to ordinary citizens. Thousands of weary peasants were inspired to fight. When the brothers followed through on their promise, their popularity grew. Eventually they wrestled control from both the Trinh and Nguyen clans and ended the Le dynasty. For a time, they reunited all of Vietnam.

However, Nguyen Anh, a prince of the Nguyen clan, was committed to regaining power. He gathered a small army and sought help from the French, who had long wanted to gain a foothold in Vietnam. After fighting for many years, Nguyen gained control of the country and established the Nguyen dynasty in 1802. This would be Vietnam's final dynasty, lasting until 1945.

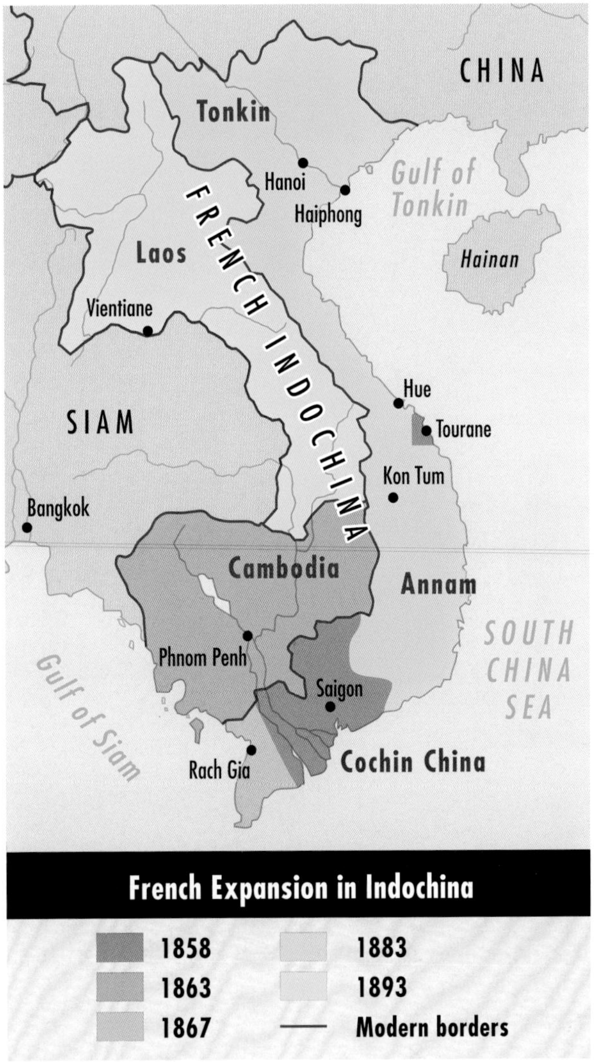

The French in Vietnam

Though the French had helped put down the Tay Son Rebellion, the Nguyen dynasty did not trust them. The French, like many other European powers at the time, wanted to establish colonies in Asia. This would help them expand their national power and obtain natural resources. Some French also promoted Christianity in Vietnam. This threatened the

The French operate cannons in 1863 during their conquest of Cochin China.

dynasty's Confucian ideas about society. Conflict between the French and the Nguyen grew as the French expanded their influence in the country, and the Nguyen repressed Christian supporters of the French.

In 1858, the French invaded Vietnam. By 1867, southern Vietnam, known as Cochin China, was under French rule. All of Vietnam was controlled by the French by 1885. They called the northern part of the country Tonkin, and the central part Annam.

The Nguyen dynasty remained in parts of the country, but it held no real power. The French were in charge of the government in Vietnam. They expanded the country's infrastructure, building new roads, ports, railroads, harbors, bridges, and factories. Most of these, however, were not used to benefit the Vietnamese people. Instead, the French developed the country to make use of its resources such as coal, rubber, and rice. They forced the Vietnamese people to work in mines and factories, paying them poorly while keeping hefty profits for themselves. Only 15 percent of Vietnamese children received any schooling during this period. Most could not read or write, and medical care was poor.

Vietnamese miners worked long days under difficult conditions.

The French treated the Vietnamese people harshly, which led to growing unrest. Despite repression by the French, the people continued to fight to win back their freedom. Various rebel groups, often with very different ideas about how the country should be run, emerged during this period. One of the most important was the Revolutionary Youth League of Vietnam, which was founded in 1925 by Nguyen Ai Quoc,

By the 1920s, Ho Chi Minh (sitting on floor) had become actively involved in the communist movement. In 1924, he attended the Congress of the Communist International.

who later changed his name to Ho Chi Minh. This group became the Indochinese Communist Party in 1930. The party urged peasants to join uprisings against the French. It also called for a more equal distribution of land and wealth throughout the country.

Japanese soldiers marched into Vietnam in 1940. The Japanese controlled Vietnam throughout World War II.

World War II

Before the Indochinese Communist Party could mount any major uprisings, World War II began. Germany invaded France, and Germany's ally Japan took over Vietnam and used it as a base for military operations. The Indochinese Communist Party

Uncle Ho

Even though Ho Chi Minh has been dead for decades, no person in Vietnam is more influential or beloved. Many Vietnamese refer to him as Uncle Ho.

Ho was named Nguyen Sinh Cung when he was born in central Vietnam in 1890. His father had been forced from his job as a teacher because he refused to learn French. Following in his father's footsteps, Ho joined student protests against the French. He then took a job on a cargo ship, which gave him an opportunity to see the world. After visiting the United States, South Africa, and Great Britain, he settled in Paris, France. There, he became committed to communism.

By 1927, Ho was living in southern China, where he helped establish the Revolutionary Youth League, Vietnam's first communist group. As he continued to inspire Vietnamese revolutionaries, the French realized that Ho was a threat to their authority in Vietnam, even though he was not in the country. They condemned him to death should he ever be captured.

In 1941, he returned quietly to his homeland, hiding in the caves of northern Vietnam. He was determined to rid Vietnam of the French. With the help of energetic young people, he formed a strong fighting force, the Viet Minh. In 1954, they finally drove the French out of Vietnam.

The peace agreement between Vietnam and France called for Vietnam to be split in two. Ho was elected president of North Vietnam, but he always believed that the country should be reunited. He didn't live long enough to see this wish come true, however. He died in 1969, and North and South Vietnam were reunited in 1976. Ho is buried in a large mausoleum (left) in the center of Hanoi. He lives on in Vietnam through his thoughts and writings, which form the philosophy of the Vietnamese Communist Party, the main political force of the country today.

saw this as an opportunity to get rid of both the Japanese and the French. In 1941, Vietnamese communists founded a special fighting force, the Viet Minh, with Ho Chi Minh as its leader.

Ho Chi Minh declared Vietnam independent in 1945. He soon traveled to France to negotiate with the French.

The Viet Minh formed an alliance with the United States, which had joined the fight against Japan and Germany in World War II. When Japan surrendered in 1945, Ho Chi Minh declared the country's independence. But the French refused to accept Vietnamese independence and fought back. They regained control of southern Vietnam, and when the Viet Minh sought help from the United States, the Americans refused. By that time, it was American policy to stop the spread of communism, so the United States sided with France, sending money to support the French war effort. This set the stage for the coming war between Vietnam and the United States.

Buildup to Battle

From 1945 until 1954, fighting continued between the Viet Minh and the French. Though the French originally fared well, things turned in favor of the Viet Minh when the

French troops parachuted into position during the Battle of Dien Bien Phu. Vietnamese forces vastly outnumbered the French and won the battle decisively.

Chinese began to fund their military. The Viet Minh were determined to win. "You can kill ten of our men for every one we kill of yours," said Ho Chi Minh in the late 1940s, "but even at those odds, you will lose and we will win."

By 1954, most of the north was controlled by the Viet Minh, while the French dominated in the south. The French were losing the will to fight and sought a way to end the war. After a major French military defeat at Dien Bien Phu in the northwest, peace talks began. A treaty was drawn up that divided Vietnam into two countries, the Democratic Republic of Vietnam (North Vietnam) and the Republic of Vietnam (South Vietnam). The treaty granted Ho Chi Minh and the Viet Minh control of North Vietnam. Ngo Dinh Diem, an important anti-communist leader, took over the government in South Vietnam. According to the treaty, there would be nationwide elections held in two years' time that would once again unify the country. But this did not happen. Instead, battles broke out between Diem's army and pro-communist forces in the south. This marked the start of the Vietnam War.

South Vietnam was extremely unstable after Diem took over. Communist forces continued to oppose his rule, as did noncommunist forces, which wanted others to lead the country. Because he knew forces opposing him would win

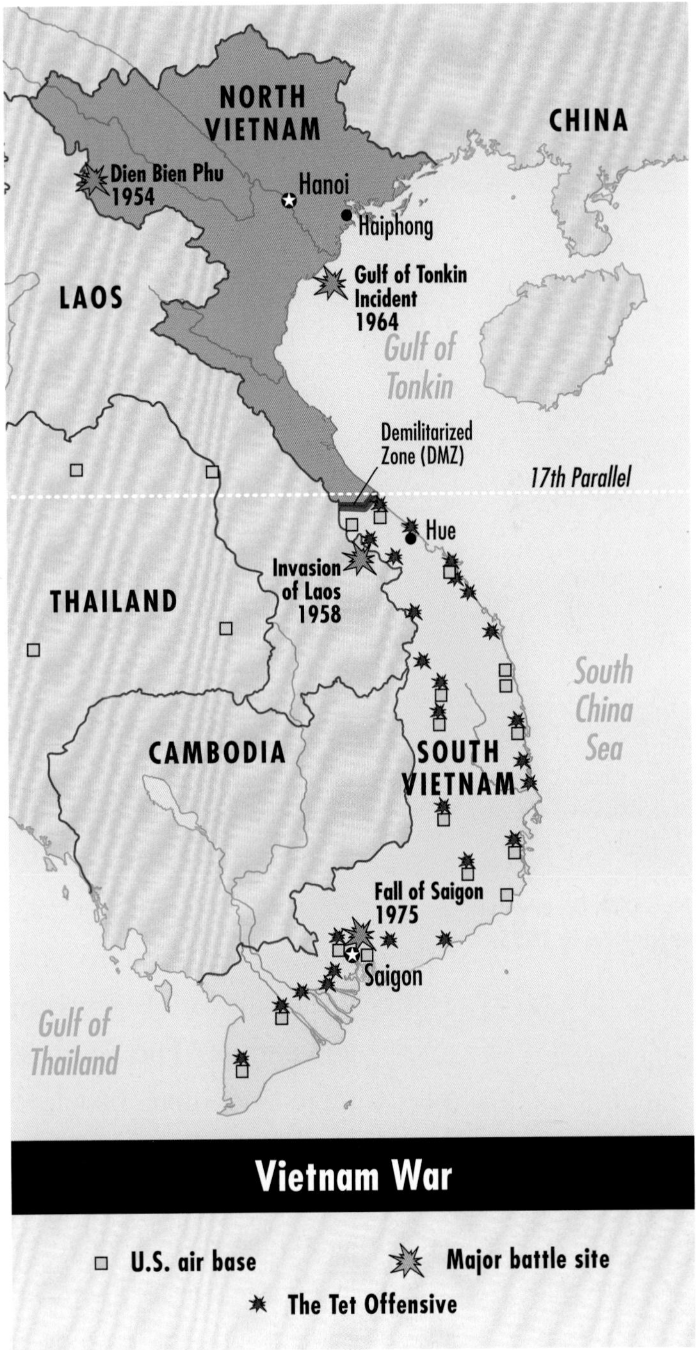

Ngo Dinh Diem waves to supporters in 1955.

the nationwide elections, Diem canceled them, with American support, and began to repress opposing political forces. This made it difficult for his government to function. It became inefficient and corrupt. The South Vietnamese economy also suffered, and more and more people became dissatisfied with Diem's rule. In 1960, a group of Diem's opponents in rural South Vietnam formed the National Liberation Front (NLF), which the North Vietnamese government supported. In 1963, a group of military leaders removed Diem from power and had him killed. This made South Vietnam even less stable.

The United States Gets Involved

American officials were worried about the growing instability in South Vietnam. In 1964, U.S. president Lyndon Johnson ordered a bombing raid on North Vietnam in the hopes of limiting the soldiers and military equipment it was sending into the south. The following year, some 3,500 American troops were also sent to assist the South Vietnamese in their fight against revolutionary forces. Most U.S. political and military leaders believed this was an easy war to win. They also believed it was necessary to help stop the spread of communism throughout Southeast Asia.

But the NLF and their northern supporters proved difficult to defeat. More and more U.S. troops were sent to Vietnam. In July 1965, seventy-five thousand American soldiers were there. Less than three years later, half a million American soldiers were in Vietnam. They joined six hundred thousand South Vietnamese soldiers in fighting revolutionary forces in South Vietnam.

Cu Chi Tunnels

The Cu Chi Tunnels are an elaborate maze of underground passageways and rooms not far from Ho Chi Minh City. The National Liberation Front (NLF) forces dug them with shovels so they could move around enemy territory and mount surprise attacks while remaining hidden. The tunnel entrances were simple holes in the ground, well hidden by leaves and branches. The tunnels had many levels and included dormitories, kitchens, hospitals, and weapon repair and storage areas. Though some of the tunnels were destroyed during the war, and more have been lost to decay in the decades since, a short length of tunnel is preserved and open to tourists.

The growing American presence, however, did not shift the tide of the war. In 1968, after years of American claims that the war was almost won, the NLF and North Vietnamese launched their largest attack. Known as the Tet Offensive because it began during Tet, the Vietnamese new year, the attack reached deep into South Vietnam's cities for the first time. Although the NLF and North Vietnamese sustained many losses, the attack was a clear sign that the war was not almost over. Opposition to the war began to grow in the United States.

NLF soldiers worked in small groups in areas they knew well. They could attack targets and then disappear into the forest.

American soldiers battle NLF forces in 1966.

The Tet Offensive increased the pressure on the U.S. government. Americans were angry. American soldiers were being killed, costs were mounting, and victory seemed unlikely. A new U.S. president, Richard Nixon, was elected in 1968. He slowly began to bring American troops home, but he also increased bombing.

In January 1973, a peace treaty was signed, and the American military finally left Vietnam. More than fifty-eight thousand U.S. soldiers had been killed. The war was supposed to be at an end. But more than one hundred thousand North Vietnamese soldiers remained in South Vietnam, and the two nations continued fighting. Two years later, the north took

The Boat People

In the years following the war, Vietnamese people crowded onto small, broken-down ships, trying to leave their nation for a better life elsewhere. Some of the so-called boat people were fleeing political persecution, while others wanted to escape poverty.

It was difficult to get out of Vietnam, but many people risked their lives trying. They first paid a large sum of money for a place on a boat. If they were caught trying to flee the country, they would probably be sent to a prison camp. About a third of those who made it on board died from disease or lack of food and water. Storms also took lives, and piracy was a problem. Entire families often traveled together, carrying all their wealth with them in the form of gold. These refugees were easy prey for pirates, who boarded the small ships to rob them. Sometimes the pirates murdered the passengers as well. Even with the dangers at sea, many Vietnamese were eager to leave their country. More than 1.5 million people tried. The boat people had to travel as far as Australia to find a place that would accept them. Hundreds of thousands ended up in the United States and Canada, eventually becoming citizens.

control of Saigon and declared victory. The communists had won. They now controlled the whole country.

The war had devastated the country. More than two million Vietnamese had died. Another three million were wounded, and American bombs and chemical sprays had damaged much of the countryside. Some villages were wiped out entirely. Twelve million people were refugees.

Reuniting Vietnam

North and South Vietnam were formally reunited on July 2, 1976. The new country was named the Socialist Republic of Vietnam. The new country faced severe problems. The country had long been focused on war. Now it had to deal with the issues that arose during peace.

North Vietnamese tanks outside the presidential palace in Saigon. On April 30, 1975, the North Vietnamese captured Saigon, ending the Vietnam War.

Neighboring countries worried that the new Vietnamese government would seek influence over them. The Cambodian communist government led several attacks against Vietnamese territory in the late 1970s. This eventually drew Vietnam into a war with Cambodia, and then with China, an ally of Cambodia. Vietnam's relationship with many of the neighboring countries deteriorated. Meanwhile, the United States and many other nations around the world restricted trade with Vietnam.

Economic Reforms

The government announced a series of economic changes in the early 1980s, which led to the *doi moi* ("new way") reforms of 1986. These reforms began to open the Vietnamese economy to the rest of the world. Relaxed regulations and government controls gave more people the opportunity to own businesses.

In 1994, the United States ended its trade restrictions with Vietnam and reestablished diplomatic relations. In 2000, Bill Clinton became the first U.S. president since Richard Nixon to visit Vietnam, and he was greeted warmly. Since then, Vietnam has improved relations with many Western nations. In 2005, Prime Minister Phan Van Khai became the first Vietnamese leader to visit the United States since the Vietnam War ended.

In recent years, Vietnamese leaders have continued to focus on boosting the economy. The government has worked to improve the lives of its citizens, and to establish itself as a presence in world trade.

Return to Vietnam

In 1975, when Hung Ba Le was five years old, he fled Vietnam on a boat. He and his family were among four hundred refugees crammed onto a small fishing vessel. In 2009, he returned to Vietnam, again on a boat. But this time, he was Commander H. B. Le, in charge of the USS *Lassen*, an American warship. Le and his crew of three hundred sailors were making a goodwill visit to Vietnam. Cheering crowds greeted Le's arrival. "This visit is a symbol of the friendship between our two nations," Le said. "To think that thirty-four years ago . . . I left here as a little boy and to come back here now, it's incredible."

Le's father had been a commander in the South Vietnamese navy. When the North took Saigon, he knew he had to get his family out of the country or they would be in danger because of his involvement in the military. He navigated the fishing boat to sea, and a U.S. Navy ship picked them up two days later.

Le and his family were brought to the United States and settled in Virginia. His father got a job bagging groceries on his second day in America. Le became a U.S. citizen in 1985 and was soon admitted to the United States Naval Academy. He is the first Vietnamese American to command a navy destroyer.

CHAPTER FIVE

One-Party Rule

Vietnam has only one political party, the Communist Party of Vietnam. People are not allowed to create other parties. All government leaders come from the Communist Party. Because of this, much of the power in Vietnam is held within the party. Though a president, prime minister, and cabinet run the government, Communist Party leaders make most decisions affecting Vietnam.

Opposite: **Young Communist Party members parade past the tomb of Ho Chi Minh in Hanoi. According to Vietnam's constitution, the Communist Party is responsible for the government's policy decisions.**

Government leaders look to Ho Chi Minh, the founder of Vietnam's Communist Party, for inspiration. Ho believed in promoting the interests of the nation's peasants and defending Vietnamese independence. The party continues to support these ideals, calling for the "struggle for peace, national independence, democracy, and social progress of the world's people." The party's stated goal is to have a close relationship with the people and give "mastery of the people over the country."

A number of organizations give citizens a chance to become involved in political life. Children may belong to the Ho Chi Minh Communist Youth Union, while many women join the Vietnam Women's Union. There are special groups

The National Flag

Vietnam's national flag consists of a yellow star on a red background. The color red symbolizes revolution and blood, and was inspired by the flag of Vietnam's Communist Party. The five points of the yellow star represent the unity of peasants, workers, soldiers, youths, and intellectuals in building socialism. This flag was adopted in 1945 by North Vietnam. Following reunification in 1976, it became the flag of Vietnam.

for certain professions, such as farmers and industrial workers. These groups organize community service projects and serve as a training ground for people who will be moving up within the Communist Party.

Running the Government

Vietnam's current constitution has been in place since 1992. It describes the structure of the government.

The main body of the Vietnamese government is the National Assembly. It has five hundred members, called deputies, who are elected to five-year terms. The National Assembly considers legislation proposed by the executive branch and citizens. It creates economic regulations and the basic foreign and domestic policies that run the country.

The head of government is the prime minister. The National Assembly elects the prime minister for a five-year term. The prime minister puts newly enacted laws into practice and ensures that the government is run correctly, the

Spotlight on the Capital

Hanoi, Vietnam's capital city, is located on the Red River in the northern part of the country. With a population of 6,472,200, it is the second-largest city in Vietnam.

Hanoi was founded during the seventh century by members of China's Sui dynasty. From 1010 to 1802, it served as the capital for many Vietnamese rulers. It was the capital of North Vietnam from 1954 until 1975, and when Vietnam was reunited in 1976, it became the nation's capital.

Today, Hanoi has many elegant and stately neighborhoods. Trees line its boulevards, and large villas serve as embassies and government office buildings. The city's outstanding landmarks include a Buddhist temple called the One-Pillar Pagoda and a fortress known as the Hanoi Citadel. Both were built about nine hundred years ago.

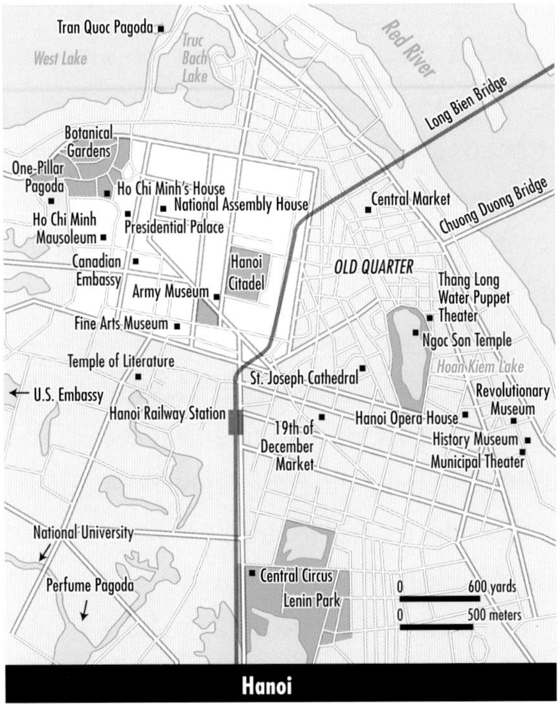

The beautiful Hanoi Opera House (top) is more than a hundred years old.

Hanoi is growing rapidly, as people from rural areas move there, hoping to make a better life for themselves. The city's growing population is contributing to its air pollution, which is among the worst in all of Southeast Asia. In the dense city center, streets are clogged with traffic, which spews pollutants and dust into the air. The pollution causes health problems for many Vietnamese, especially children. City leaders are searching for ways to improve the city's air quality. They are considering building a subway system to reduce traffic.

Truong Tan Sang is both the president and the leading member of the Communist Party in Vietnam.

country remains stable, and the constitution is observed. Nguyen Tan Dung has been the prime minister of Vietnam since 2006. He was elected to his second term in 2011.

The prime minister heads a cabinet, which includes deputy prime ministers and state organization heads. The prime minister appoints the cabinet members, who direct areas of national concern such as water conservation, forestry, and agriculture. They also supervise the work of local governments.

The president of Vietnam is the head of state. Members of the National Assembly elect the president to a five-year term. The president's responsibilities include leading the country's military. The president also has the right to declare a state of emergency or war. Truong Tan Sang was elected president in 2011.

The vice president assists the president. He or she is nominated by the president and elected by the National Assembly.

National Government of Vietnam

Executive Branch

President

Vice President

Prime Minister

Cabinet

Legislative Branch

National Assembly
(500 members)

Judicial Branch

Supreme
People's Court

Provincial
Municipal Courts

District Courts

Military Courts

The Justice System

District courts are the lowest courts in Vietnam's justice system. There are more than five hundred of them in the country. Decisions made in district courts may be appealed to higher courts called provincial municipal courts.

The Supreme People's Court is the highest court in Vietnam. It reviews decisions made at the city or county level. It also handles cases that involve crimes such as treason. The

National Assembly elects the chief judge of the Supreme People's Court. The president nominates and dismisses the other judges on the court.

Local Politics

Vietnam has fifty-eight provinces and five municipalities. These are further divided into towns, districts, and villages, which are led locally by people's councils. There is resistance in some regions to the decisions made by the national government, especially in some of the more remote tribal regions.

The National Anthem

Nguyen Van Cao wrote the words and music to "Tien Quan Ca" ("Song of the Marching Army") in 1944. The song was officially adopted as Vietnam's national anthem when the country was reunified following the Vietnam War.

English translation

Soldiers of Vietnam, we go forward,
With the one will to save our Fatherland.
Our hurried steps are sounding on the long and arduous road.
Our flag, red with the blood of victory, bears the spirit of our country.
The distant rumbling of the guns mingles with our marching song.
The path to glory passes over the bodies of our foes.
Overcoming all hardships, together we build our resistance bases.
Ceaselessly for the people's cause we struggle,
Hastening to the battlefield!
Forward! All together advancing!

A Vietnamese woman votes in the 2011 elections. Although many Vietnamese go to the polls, elections have little meaning because only communists are allowed to hold power.

Protests

Some Vietnamese are unhappy with the current communist government. They feel that Vietnamese people should have more individual freedoms. Many people are in the nation's jails simply for expressing their political and religious views. People who try to form any political party that would oppose the Communist Party can be arrested. Those who write articles and blogs against communism or give interviews with foreign radio and television programs can also be prosecuted. Workers who try to organize protests or strikes are accused of "disrupting security." Most serve several years in prison, and then have many of their rights stripped away even after they are freed. As other nations around the world take note of these human rights violations, they are putting more pressure on the Vietnamese government to give the people greater freedom.

CHAPTER SIX

A Growing Economy

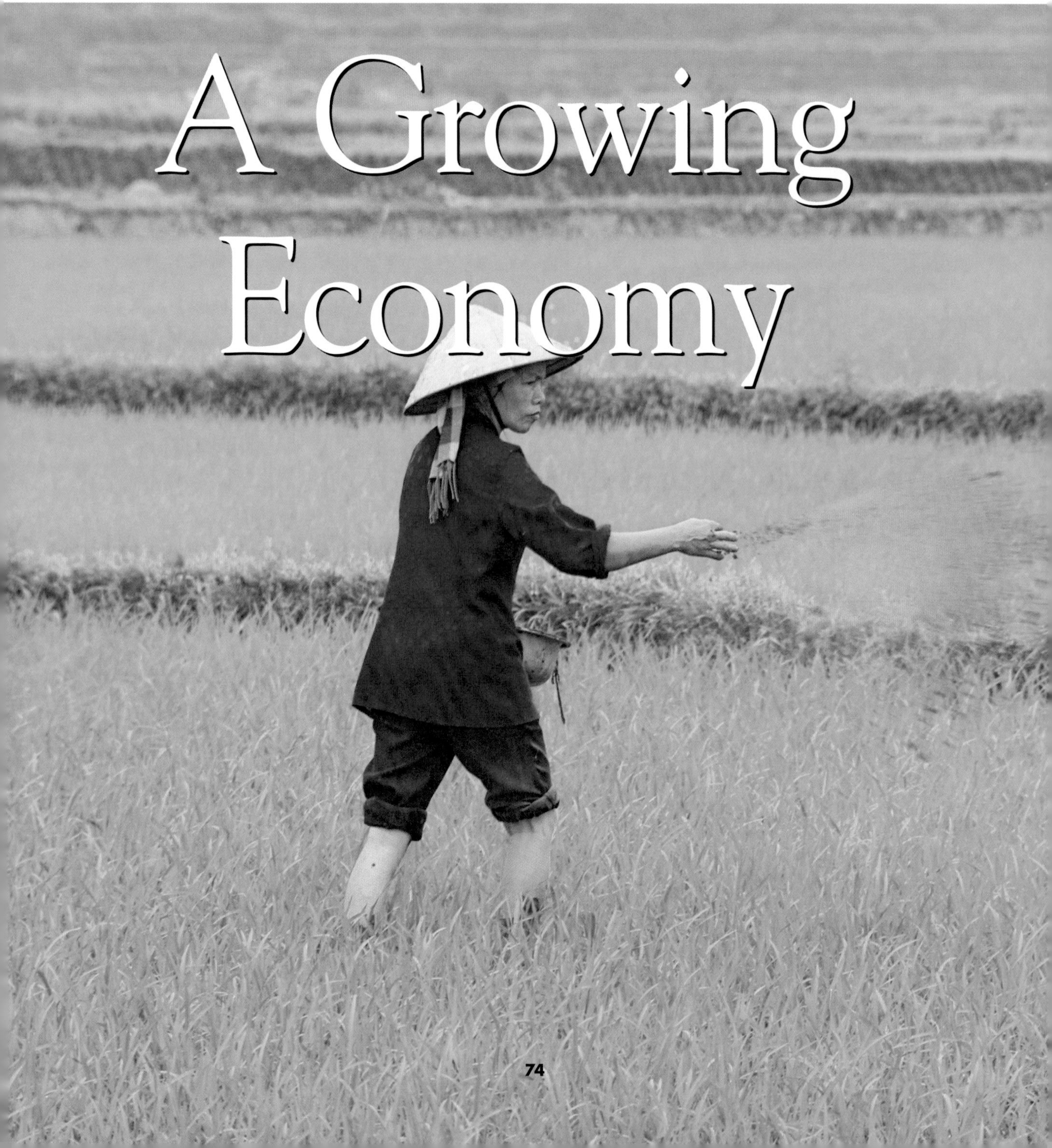

VIETNAM HAS HISTORICALLY BEEN AN AGRICULTURAL nation. For centuries, people produced the food needed to feed their families. In more recent times, they might have had a little extra food to sell at the market. Some people also made their livings in mining or trade.

Opposite: **A Vietnamese farmer works in a rice field. Vietnam is the world's second-largest exporter of rice.**

In 1976, Vietnam became a communist nation. In communist countries, the government controls the economy and runs businesses. Any profits are shared with citizens. Sometimes that works, but sometimes it can cause problems. In Vietnam, bad business deals, poor management, and corruption brought hard times. Under communism, the quality of goods and services declined, and incomes dropped.

A change in this practice was needed. It came in 1986, with a reform movement called *doi moi*. Under this plan, the government returned businesses to private citizens and encouraged more international trade. Though the government still maintains control over most business and industry,

Fruits and vegetables grow well in Vietnam. The markets are filled with cucumbers, spinach, eggplants, and much more.

it has lifted many restrictions. Since the reforms have been in effect, Vietnam's economy has improved greatly.

The percentage of people living in poverty has gone down significantly. In 1992, it was 58 percent of the population. That amount dropped to 29 percent in 2002, and by 2010 it had dropped to 11 percent. Vietnam's economy grew by 7 percent each year from 2000 to 2005, making it one of the world's fastest-growing economies. In the years that followed, the country's economy remained strong, even as much of the world was dealing with financial hardships. Many economists consider Vietnam a rising star in Asia.

Industry

Industry is the main force in Vietnam's economy, making up about 41 percent of the country's income and employing about 20 percent of Vietnamese workers. Vietnam's industrial output is growing as the country opens up to more investment and trade with other nations.

Mining is a large part of Vietnam's economy, and coal is a major export. The Vietnamese also mine phosphate, iron, tin, and chromium. Another important industry is food processing. Seafood is often processed before it is exported. Coffee and tea are also processed in Vietnam. Both silk and cement are produced for export, as are fertilizers, steel, rubber, and clothing. Manufactured products include electrical equipment, machine tools, and bicycles.

Hundreds of thousands of Vietnamese work in clothing factories. Vietnam exports more clothes to the United States than any other nation except China.

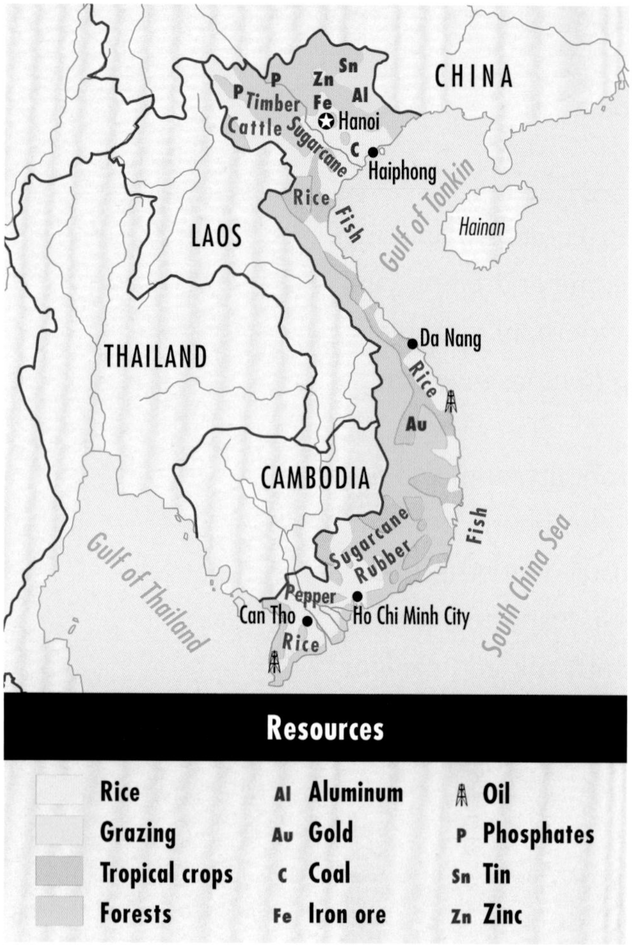

The United States is the largest consumer of Vietnamese products. In 2010, about 20 percent of Vietnamese exports went to the United States. Japan and China are also major trade partners for Vietnam. Each accounts for about 10 percent of Vietnamese exports.

Agriculture

More than half the Vietnamese labor force works in agriculture. Rice is the main crop in Vietnam, as it has been for centuries. Large areas of the country's lowlands are devoted to rice production. Other crops grown in Vietnam include peanuts, corn, sweet potatoes, sugarcane, cassava, bananas, and coconuts. Coffee is grown in the highlands.

Into Space

Vietnam is developing a space program that will launch satellites to assist with functions such as weather forecasting. The country launched its first satellite in 2008, and another is slated to go into orbit in 2014. A space center being built near Hanoi will be the center of research and production for more satellites.

What Vietnam Grows, Makes, and Mines

Agriculture (2009)	
Rice	38,895,500 metric tons
Sugarcane	15,246,400 metric tons
Cassava	8,556,900 metric tons
Manufacturing (2004 value sold)	
Foods and beverages	156.1 trillion Vietnamese dong
Cement, bricks, and pottery	46.2 trillion dong
Paints, soaps, and pharmaceuticals	43.9 trillion dong
Mining and Quarrying	
Petroleum (2007)	105,460,000 barrels
Coal (2007)	45,328,000 metric tons
Phosphate rock (2009)	1,896,000 metric tons

Fishing is also important to the Vietnamese economy. Along the coast, Vietnamese catch or raise shrimp, crab, squid, and lobster.

Services

About one-quarter of Vietnamese workers are employed in service industries. This includes banking, education, trade, health care, and much more.

Tourism is one of the fastest growing service industries. Vietnam has beautiful natural settings, interesting history, and lively cities. But until the doi moi reforms were in place, the country did not do much to attract tourists. That has begun to change. Large, elegant hotels have been built. Tour operators are now eager to guide visitors on various trips, such as snorkeling in Ha Long Bay, bicycling in the central highlands, or boating in the Mekong Delta. Hungry travelers can find inexpensive food sold along the roadside and delicious gour-

Tourists relax in a boat on Ha Long Bay.

Money Facts

The dong is the basic unit of currency in Vietnam. Coins come in values of 500, 1,000, 2,000, and 5,000 dong. Paper money comes in values of 10,000, 20,000, 50,000, 100,000, 200,000, and 500,000 dong. Each denomination is a different color. The 20,000-dong bill, for example, is blue, while the 200,000-dong bill is brownish-red. All denominations of Vietnamese bills show Ho Chi Minh on the front. The backs of the bills show a variety of scenes, including the covered bridge in Hoi An, the city of Hue, Ha Long Bay, and Ho Chi Minh's birthplace in Kim Lien. In June 2012, US$1.00 was equal to 21,000 dong.

met meals offered in fancy restaurants. Most beaches are clean and easy to get to, with plenty of services available. Visitors can enjoy many traditional arts, concerts, and theater productions. All across the country, handicrafts are for sale. In 2011, six million international tourists visited Vietnam.

Transportation

Vietnam's mountainous land makes transportation difficult between the north and the south. Highways and train tracks can run only along the coast. More roads are being built, but many remain unpaved. In the Mekong Delta and the Red River delta, river travel is common. The country has several large ports, including those at Ho Chi Minh City, Da Nang, and Haiphong. Ho Chi Minh City and Hanoi have major airports.

CHAPTER SEVEN

People and Language

Despite Vietnam's long history of struggle and civil war, the Vietnamese people remain warm and friendly, even to visitors from nations that were once their enemies. Many Vietnamese today show great forgiveness and a welcoming spirit.

Opposite: **Bicycles and motorcycles crowd the streets of Hanoi.**

Vietnam is a crowded country, and the Vietnamese people have learned to live closely together. In 2011, the population of Vietnam was 91,519,289. This number is growing rapidly—by about 1 percent a year. This means the population increases by about a million people every year. Vietnam is the thirteenth most populated country in the world, but only the sixty-fifth largest in area. Much of Vietnam is too steep or swampy for people to inhabit, so the Vietnamese are crowded onto about 20 percent of the land.

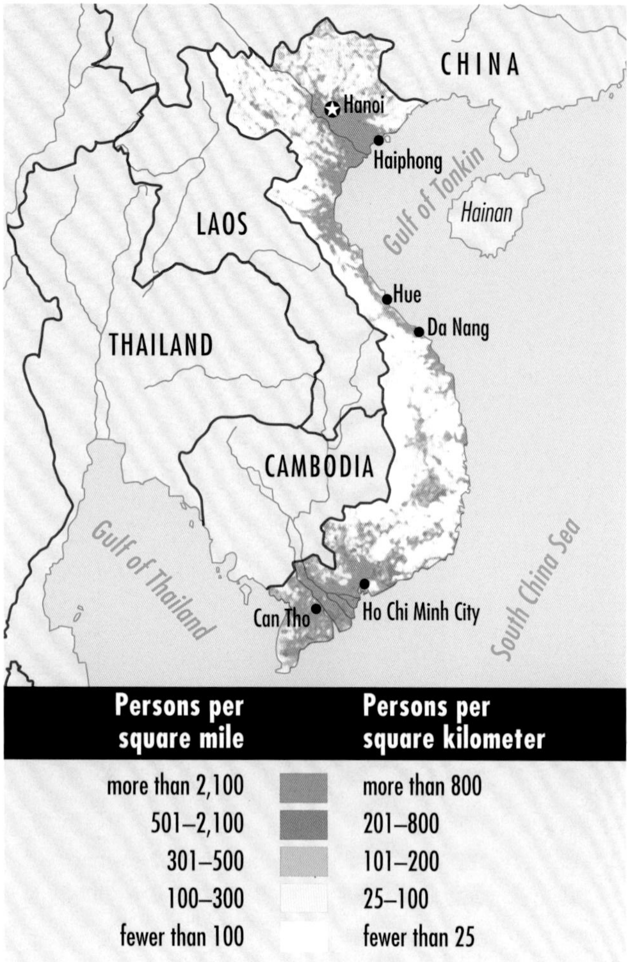

The history of Chinese rule also plays a role in the Vietnamese people's ability to live peacefully in tight quarters. The Chinese brought Confucianism to Vietnam, and Confucian beliefs emphasize the importance of being part of a group over being simply an individual. In Confucianism, the best interests of the group are more important than the wishes of just one person. All members of the group are responsible for one another. This philosophy eases the tensions of living so closely with others.

Ethnic Groups

There are fifty-four different ethnic groups in Vietnam. The largest group is the Viet, or Kinh, who make up about 86 percent of the population.

Population of Major Cities (2009 est.)

Ho Chi Minh City	7,396,446
Hanoi	6,472,200
Haiphong	1,907,705
Can Tho	1,187,089
Da Nang	887,069

The Kinh originated in what is now northern Vietnam. They are descendants of the Dong Son people of the Red River delta region. The Dong Son people were of Chinese and Indonesian origin. About two thousand years ago, they mixed with others who had recently come into the area from Thailand, Indonesia, and China. Their descendants became the Kinh. As their numbers grew, they spread south along the coast and into the Mekong River delta. The Kinh lived near water, which they needed to grow their staple food, rice. Today, rice is still an important part of their diet, and the deltas of the Mekong and Red Rivers are still the most populated areas in the country.

While the Kinh dominated the coastal regions, groups known as hill tribes made their homes in the northern and central highlands. This is challenging terrain, with steep hillsides, thick forests, and rushing rivers, so the villages remained isolated from one another. Each hill tribe developed a culture all its own. Even today, each tribe's clothing is distinctive. People who live in the region can usually tell where a person

Ethnic Groups in Vietnam (2009)

Viet Kinh	85.7%
Tay	1.9%
Thai	1.8%
Muong	1.5%
Khmer	1.5%
Hmong	1.2%
Nung	1.1%
Other	5.3%

About half a million people of the Dao ethnic group live in Vietnam. Some Dao people typically wear dark jackets and red turbans.

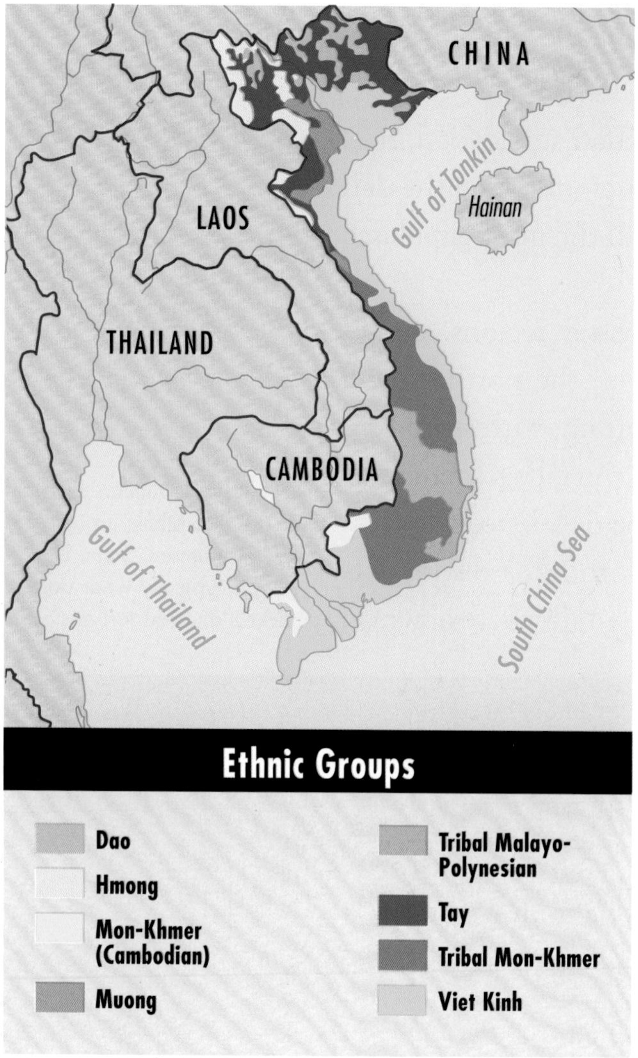

is from by what he or she is wearing. Most members of hill tribes are farmers. They grow fruits and vegetables and raise pigs and chickens to feed their families. They also grow some crops for sale, such as tobacco, cotton, and tea. New roads have made it easier to reach the hill tribes' villages, and many tourists are now making the journey. Visitors enjoy the colorful markets, lovely scenery, and slower pace of life there.

The Tay people are the largest minority group in Vietnam. They live on the lower slopes of mountains in northern Vietnam. Tay clothes are generally died blue. Women wear skirts that are split up the right side. Their shirts have narrow sleeves and five buttons below the arm.

The Hmong people are the most remote of the hill tribes. They live in the northern highlands, as well as in the mountains of Laos, Thailand, and southern China. Hmong people typically wear clothing with colorful embroidery.

Unlike most minorities in Vietnam, the ethnic Chinese, called the Hoa, live in the lowlands and in major cities. Many Hoa people own small businesses.

Language

Vietnamese is the official language of Vietnam. Different versions, or dialects, of Vietnamese are spoken in different parts of the country. The second most common language is English, and some older people speak French. Many of the country's ethnic groups have their own languages as well.

The Hmong people live throughout Southeast Asia.

Body Language

Body language is an important part of communication in Vietnam. It can show respect, agreement, and friendliness, or it can be a sign of contempt and disrespect. In some cases, gestures that mean one thing in English-speaking countries mean something very different in Vietnam.

Vietnamese students avoid looking directly into the eyes of a teacher. This shows respect. Making eye contact with the teacher signals a challenge. In the United States and Canada, a student who avoids eye contact

with a teacher may be thought to be hiding something or may be viewed as being disrespectful.

In Vietnam, a smile is an expression of apology for a minor offense or a way to show appreciation for a small gesture. No words need to be spoken. In other cultures, people often expect to hear the words, "I'm sorry," or "thank you."

In Vietnamese culture, men may shake hands as a friendly greeting, but men and women rarely shake hands with each other. Two people of the same sex may walk hand in hand or arm in arm, a simple sign of friendship.

Having a conversation with your arms crossed might indicate disagreement in the United States and Canada. But in Vietnam, it is a sign of respect. It is a sign of disrespect, however, to pat someone on the back in Vietnam, especially if a younger person pats an older person.

The Written Language

Until about 1900, Chinese was the language of government and high culture in Vietnam. Each Chinese character represents one syllable, which was considered one word. That is why it is common in Vietnam today to see the name of Hanoi, for example, written as Ha Noi.

In the 1600s, Catholic missionaries from Europe entered Vietnam, hoping to spread their faith. They developed a system of Roman letters, similar to the English alphabet, which allowed them to write down the Vietnamese language. This system, called *quoc-ngu* (meaning "national language"), replaced Chinese in the early 1900s. Today, 94 percent of Vietnamese can read and write quoc-ngu.

A sign on a beach near Da Nang asks visitors to clean up after themselves.

Speaking Vietnamese

chào ban	hello, good-bye
Ban khóc không?	How are you?
lám on	please
cám on	thank you
Bà tên là gì?	What's your name?
Tôi tên là . . .	My name is . . .

A security guard reads a newspaper in Ho Chi Minh City. Most daily newspapers are in the Vietnamese language, although there are several in English and one in French.

Education

The Vietnamese place a strong emphasis on education. Despite the long civil war that disrupted the lives of all Vietnamese, 94 percent of the people can read and write.

Children are required to attend school for nine years. In primary school, which runs for five years starting at age six, children study subjects such as math, science, history, the

Quoc-ngu

Quoc-ngu is the written form of the Vietnamese language. It uses the same letters as English, although it does not include *f*, *j*, *w*, and *z*. Letters sometimes appear with diacritical marks (signs such as accent marks), which indicate how the letter should be pronounced. A falling diagonal accent mark above a letter, for example, indicates that the syllable should be spoken in a falling tone, ending in the speaker's lower range. A small curved line above a letter means that it is a short syllable, with the voice beginning in midrange, stopping, and then quickly rising. The diacritical marks can indicate six different tones. An example is the word *ma*. Depending on the tone, it can mean "tomb," "ghost," "but," "mother," "rice seedling," or "horse." Including all the diacritical marks, quoc-ngu actually has twenty-seven consonants and twelve vowels.

Vietnamese is considered among the most difficult languages to learn to speak. Most Vietnamese people appreciate any effort foreigners make to learn their language, even if it is just a few phrases.

Vietnamese language, ethics, art, and music. In secondary school, which runs for four years, children study subjects such as literature, chemistry, biology, physics, economics, politics, and a foreign language, usually English. Students who are going to continue on to college attend an additional three years of secondary school.

Vietnam has a total of 163 universities. The largest is Vietnam National University, which has campuses in Hanoi and Ho Chi Minh City. Many Vietnamese college students also study abroad, in countries such as the United States and Japan.

For most Vietnamese children, school lasts for a half day.

CHAPTER EIGHT

Blended Religions

SPIRITUALITY IS AN IMPORTANT PART OF VIETNAMESE life. For most Vietnamese people, their traditions are a blend of parts from several faiths, including Buddhism, Confucianism, and Daoism. These three belief systems have been central to Vietnamese culture for centuries. They have merged with ancient Vietnamese customs of worshipping national heroes and ancestors.

Opposite: **Several Buddhist temples lie in the Marble Mountains overlooking Da Nang.**

Because the people's religious beliefs are drawn from so many different sources, it is not easy to say which religion is the most common in Vietnam. In fact, most Vietnamese say they do not belong to any religion. But their behaviors, customs, and history tell of a culture with a strong belief in the spirit world.

Altars in Vietnamese homes often include food, flowers, and incense.

Nearly all homes contain an altar where people frequently pray and make offerings to ancestors. At these altars they may ask for help in school or business, or give thanks for a good harvest or hunt. Sometimes they ask their ancestors for guidance in family matters, and sometimes they mark the anniversary of a birth or death. No matter what religion Vietnamese people follow, they usually honor their ancestors in this way. Many Vietnamese fear their ancestors would become angry if they did not make offerings to them.

Celebrating the New Year

Traditionally, the Vietnamese used a lunar calendar, which is based on the cycles of the moon. Tet Nguyen Dan, often referred to simply as Tet, marks the beginning of the lunar new year. The Vietnamese celebrate this three-day holiday each spring as a sign of rebirth, and ancestor worship plays an important role in the festivities.

Preparations begin early, as people clean up their family tombs, pay their debts, and decorate their homes. Streets are decorated with flowers and lights. During the festival, people spend most of their time with family. They share delicious meals, exchange gifts, and attend parades, concerts, and fairs. They eat candied fruit and fancy chocolates. A special treat is *banh tet*, a mixture of rice, bean paste, and pork wrapped in banana leaves and boiled.

The most important part of Tet is worshipping ancestors. People light large sticks of incense, hoping the scented smoke will drift toward the heavens, attracting the attention of their ancestors and calling them back for the earthly celebrations. Offerings of food, drink, incense, and flowers are left for the ancestors on the family altars found in every home.

Buddhism

Buddhism forms the basis for the spiritual lives of the majority of Vietnamese people. Pagodas—Buddhist shrines— are common, and Buddhist festivals are a part of the nation's holiday calendar.

Buddhists have a lifelong goal of enlightenment. They strive to understand life and their place in it. They try to live peacefully, with care and concern for other living beings. They also try to limit their desire for material items.

The Four Noble Truths form the basis of the Buddhist faith. These truths are that people are born to suffer; that suffering is caused by the desire for pleasure and possessions; that suffering ends when people give up their attachments to all things; and that the Eightfold Path shows the way to end this attachment. The Eightfold Path is a way of developing wisdom and living correctly. It includes the traits that will lead

The Buddha

Buddhism was founded by Siddhartha Gautama, who lived during the sixth century BCE in the area that is now Nepal. His family was wealthy, but he gave up his comfortable living to try to understand why the world is filled with suffering. He spent many years meditating, until he came to the belief that suffering comes from greed and other desires. He believed that people could move past those desires, and that when they do, they achieve a state of bliss known as nirvana, or enlightenment. Gautama became known as the Buddha, which means "the enlightened one." He devoted the rest of his life to spreading the principles of Buddhism.

Buddhist monks in Vietnam typically wear yellow robes.

to enlightenment. These are right thought, right speech, right action, right understanding, right livelihood, right effort, right mindfulness, and right concentration.

Most Buddhists in Vietnam belong to a branch of the religion called Mahayana Buddhism. They believe that some people are bodhisattvas, people who have achieved enlightenment but choose to remain on earth to help others reach salvation. "A bodhisattva is someone who has compassion within himself or herself and who is able to make another person smile or help someone suffer less," says Vietnamese monk Thich Nhat Hanh. "Every one of us is capable of this."

People pray and light incense at temples across Vietnam.

The belief in bodhisattvas meshes easily with the Vietnamese practice of ancestor worship. People can consider their ancestors to be bodhisattvas. Different faiths exist side by side in the hearts of the Vietnamese.

Confucianism

Many people do not consider Confucianism a religion. Instead, it is often called a philosophy, but one that includes principles and values that people use to guide their actions. Confucianism emerged from the thinking of a teacher named Confucius, who lived around 500 BCE in China. Confucius was an official in the court of the emperor during a time of unrest in China. To help calm the people and restore order, he wrote a set of guidelines based on the ideas of obedience to family, society, and government. Confucianism stresses giving up personal desires and focusing on what is best for other people.

Many emperors and kings liked Confucianism, since it promotes obedience and made it easier for them to rule. When the Chinese invaded Vietnam, they were eager to introduce Confucianism to the region as a way to control the people. But Confucianism also teaches that rulers must lead by good example and treat their subjects with kindness. The Vietnamese people took this to heart as well. When the Chinese treated them cruelly, the Vietnamese believed that the teachings of Confucius allowed them to rebel.

In Vietnamese culture, turtles are a symbol of stability and a long life. Hundreds of years ago at the Confucian Temple of Literature in Hanoi, the names of outstanding students were carved on monuments that rise from the backs of statues of turtles.

Today, many Confucian values are still apparent in Vietnam. Most Vietnamese consider what is best for their families and communities when making personal decisions. They give great respect to their elders, teachers, and political leaders.

Daoism

A belief in the spirit world is the main focus of Daoism, a religion that began in China during the sixth century BCE. Daoism is based on intuition, or basic understanding of things

A statue of the god Tran Vu sits in the Daoist Quan Thanh Temple in Hanoi. The second-largest bronze statue in Vietnam, it is 13 feet (4 m) tall.

that are invisible and cannot be taught. Daoists believe in living compassionately and peacefully. By developing these qualities, along with a personal spiritual quest, they can achieve what is called ultimate stillness.

Vietnamese at a Daoist temple in Ho Chi Minh City. Daoism encourages people to live in harmony with the world.

One of the main components of Daoism is a belief in the balance of the universe. According to this idea, everything in nature has an opposite that balances it and creates harmony. This concept is sometimes known as yin and yang. Daoists strive to keep balance in all their actions.

Like Confucianism, Daoism came to Vietnam during the period of Chinese rule. For several centuries, both belief systems were equally popular in Vietnam. By the 1400s, Daoism

ALAMEDA FREE LIBRARY

The Jade Emperor is the supreme god in Daoism.

began to decline in Vietnam, and today there are few people who follow Daosim only. It still exists in some form, however, as part of the blend of beliefs followed by many Vietnamese.

Tam Giao

Many Buddhists weave teachings from Confucianism and Daoism into their beliefs. This practice is called Tam Giao, or Three Religions, and it is common in Vietnam. In keeping with Tam Giao, most Vietnamese temples contain items particular to all three beliefs. There are statues of the Buddha, as well as statues of such Daoist gods as Ngoc Hoang, the Jade Emperor. A side altar often holds photos of the deceased relatives of people who live in the community. Visitors to a temple often pray to several gods or burn incense as an offering to the spirits.

Cao Dai and Hoa Hao

In the early twentieth century, two religions were founded in southern Vietnam. In 1926, Ngo Van Chieu founded Cao Dai, which means "Kingdom of Heaven." Chieu stated that he was passing on teachings he had received directly from God. Cao Dai teaches that there is only one God. Followers of Cao Dai practice nonviolence, vegetarianism, and the worship of ancestors. They hope to rejoin God in heaven upon their deaths. There are more than two million followers of Cao Dai worldwide. Nearly all of them live in Vietnam.

Cao Dai worshippers fill a temple near Ho Chi Minh City. The religion's name comes from words that mean "high" and "palace," the place where God reigns.

Religions of Vietnam

It is difficult to state specific percentages of the religious beliefs of the people of Vietnam because people combine elements of many different faiths. The percentages shown represent those who follow only one faith. Those who blend faiths are listed as "other."

Buddhist	9.3%
Catholic	6.7%
Hoa Hao	1.5%
Cao Dai	1.1%
Protestant	0.5%
Muslim	0.1%
Other	80.8%

Hoa Hao was founded in 1939 by Huynh Phu So. Hoa Hao is based on Buddhism. Huynh Phu So formed the religion with the goal of saving people from suffering while protecting the nation of Vietnam. He stressed that people should practice Buddhist worship in their homes rather than in temples. He preferred to give charity to the poor rather than to spend money on building elaborate pagodas.

Today, most of Hoa Hao's approximately two million followers live in Vietnam. In parts of the Mekong Delta region where the religion began, some 90 percent of local residents practice Hoa Hao.

There are about 1,700 Hoa Hao monks in Vietnam.

The French built Catholic churches, such as this one in Da Lat in the central highlands, in a European style.

Christianity and Other Religions

Portuguese and Spanish missionaries who came to Vietnam's northern coast during the 1600s were the first people to bring Christianity to the region. In the century that followed, European missionaries established several permanent missions. In many ways, Christianity's teachings are not part of traditional Vietnamese culture. For example, Christianity does

Boys pray at a mass in Ho Chi Minh City.

not allow a belief in more than one god. While Confucianism promotes the idea that people must be obedient to their rulers, Christianity teaches that all people are equal. In the 1800s, some Vietnamese Christians fought for France during its conquest of Vietnam. As a result, many Christians in Vietnam were persecuted, and some were killed.

Today, nearly six million Catholics live in Vietnam. The nation is also home to about five hundred thousand Protestants. They belong to a variety of churches, including Baptist, Assemblies of God, and Mennonite.

Several other religions have attracted small followings in Vietnam. Hinduism was first introduced to Vietnam by Indian explorers. The Champa people of the Mekong Delta were strongly influenced by Hinduism, and about eighty-five thousand Chams today consider themselves Hindu. About sixty-five thousand Muslims, followers of the religion Islam, also live in Vietnam. Most live in the southeast part of the country.

A Vietnamese Muslim reads the Qur'an, the holy book of Islam, in Ho Chi Minh City.

CHAPTER NINE

Culture in Transition

THE CULTURE OF VIETNAM IS IN TRANSITION. Some people are working to preserve the country's unique traditions and customs, while others are speeding into the future without looking back. Vietnam is a nation alive with music, dance, and theater, so everyone can find something to satisfy their tastes.

Opposite: **A woman plays a trung, a traditional bamboo xylophone, at the Ho Chi Minh City Opera House. Trungs can be played either flat or vertically.**

Music

The world's oldest-known instrument hails from Vietnam's central highlands. Called a *dan da*, it is similar to a xylophone. A dan da is made of a set of six or more rocks of various shapes and sizes. The performer hits the rocks with a wooden mallet, producing a ringing tone.

Dan das are still in use today, along with such traditional instruments as coin clappers, flutes made from hollow bamboo stalks, and gongs. Large orchestras often perform the folk tunes that were once played using these instruments. Vietnam has also produced many jazz, reggae, techno, rap, hip-hop, and rock musicians.

As the country becomes more open to international influences, the music industry is growing. There is a music video station on television, and the number of music clubs is increasing. Japanese, Korean, and American influences are particularly strong.

Many popular Vietnamese artists also look to their own traditions for inspiration. Some add traditional elements to their music. For example, songs might include a drumbeat similar to traditional drumbeats heard in the central highlands. Some Vietnamese artists also choose to use their music to make a

Bands such as the Khac Chi Ensemble highlight traditional Vietnamese instruments.

personal statement about life in Vietnam. Trinh Cong Son was a legendary songwriter during the 1960s and 1970s. He wrote hundreds of love songs and songs about the Vietnam War, and he supported the country's reunification. Hundreds of thousands of people attended his funeral when he died in 2001.

Rock music was introduced into Vietnam by U.S. soldiers during the Vietnam War. Today, it remains popular, particularly in the south.

The Power of Music

Vietnamese musicians who speak out against the government in their art put themselves in danger. Some have even been arrested.

Viet Khang was born into a poor family in 1973. He always loved music, and he became a singer, songwriter, and drummer. As he traveled around Vietnam, he saw many injustices and widespread poverty. He worried about his nation's future. In response to the problems he witnessed, in April 2011 he and other young Vietnamese formed a group called Patriotic Youth. This group of young students, artists, and professionals speaks out for social justice through blogs, Web sites, and art.

Even though he knew he could get in trouble, in December 2011, Viet Khang released two patriotic protest songs over the Internet. In the song "Where Is My Vietnam?" he asks his fellow citizens to look at their government's injustices and take responsibility for Vietnam's future. In "Who Are You?" he wonders about the harsh treatment of protesters. "May I ask, who are you to keep me from protesting for love of this country whose people have endured far too much!" he sings. Just after the release of these songs, Vietnam's security police arrested Viet Khang and jailed him without charge. His arrest brought attention to the many political prisoners in Vietnam.

Imperial court dances developed hundreds of years ago for the entertainment of the kings and nobles. Today, they are still performed at festivals.

Theater

For more than a thousand years, a form of opera called *hat cheo* has been performed in the Red River valley. Originally performed by peasants, hat cheo was a way that peasants could make fun of their masters. The stories are usually funny and are told through dance, song, and mime. By now the plots are well known, though the actors usually add their own twists. Hat cheo performances are still popular, especially in Hanoi. Audience members sometimes beat on drums to show their approval.

Hat tuong, another form of opera, was brought to Vietnam by the Chinese about eight hundred years ago. At the time, it was performed only for royalty. The stories in hat tuong are usually epic historic tales, which stress the lessons of Confucius.

Thang Long Water Puppet Theater

The Thang Long Water Puppet Theater in Hanoi offers a glimpse into the nation's past, showcasing an art form that dates back a thousand years in the Red River delta. *Mua roi nuoc,* or water puppetry, was created by farmers as a way to teach and entertain their children. The shows depict ordinary life, as well as scenes from fables, myths, and legends. Later, the shows were performed on the delta's rice paddies to give thanks for harvests and to entertain members of the ruling family.

Performers kept the techniques behind water puppetry secret for centuries. The skills were passed down from older to younger men within families. Women were not allowed to learn this art form for fear they would spread secrets to their husbands' families.

Today, the puppet shows are performed on a stage covered with water. The puppeteers move the puppets across the watery surface using poles, rods, and strings hidden under the water. Because the puppets are often heavy and hard to maneuver, it often takes two or more puppeteers standing knee-deep in the water to control each puppet. Their skill is extraordinary. They make the puppets perform actions such as blowing smoke and throwing balls. Vietnamese folk music, performed with traditional xylophones, gongs, bamboo flutes, and bronze drums, plays in the background while the puppets glide and dance over the water.

Vietnam's most popular form of theater today is *hat cai luong*, which began in the Mekong Delta one hundred years ago. Hat cai luong mixes Vietnamese songs, Chinese operatic theater, and French popular music. The dialogue is usually spoken, but the music sets the mood. The dramas often deal with difficult themes of love and the challenge of balancing traditional ways with modern times.

Dancers perform at the Royal Theater in Hue.

A girl reads a book at a book stall in Hanoi.

The Written Word

The most popular form of literature in Vietnam is the poem. Many poems are memorized, shared aloud, and handed down through generations. One epic poem is especially beloved. It is *Kim-Van-Kieu* (*The Tale of Kieu*), written by Nguyen Du, who lived from 1765 to 1820. Many consider it to be the most important work of Vietnamese literature. It tells the story of a beautiful, talented young girl who struggles against many hardships to protect her family and its honor.

Other popular poems describe the Vietnamese love of country and the willingness of people to fight foreign invaders. Many Vietnamese write poetry and share it with people who are facing hardships such as poverty, illness, or persecution.

Arts and Crafts

Vietnam has strong traditions in stone and wood carving, pottery, and other crafts. Most traditional crafts in Vietnam developed in rural areas. Families would sell crafts to earn a bit more money. Over time, the residents of some villages developed special skills and focused on one particular type of craft. This was the start of the craft villages that continue to flourish today. These villages specialize in works ranging from bamboo birdcages to wood carvings to woven silk. The craft villages, many of which are near Hanoi, are now popular tourist attractions. In 2003, Ho Chi Minh City set up new craft villages in poor areas of the city. Though these did not develop in the traditional way, they have helped residents earn more money.

Wood carving is one of the many crafts practiced in Vietnam's craft villages.

Soccer Hero

One of Vietnam's most exciting young soccer stars is Le Cong Vinh, who plays for the Hanoi team and is a member of the Vietnamese national team. Vinh, who was born in 1985, is considered one of the best players in Southeast Asia. He has frequently been the top scorer in the Vietnam Football Federation, and three times he has won the Vietnamese Golden Ball, which is awarded to the league's best player of the year.

Sports

The most popular spectator sport in Vietnam is soccer, also known as football. Many cities have teams in the Vietnam Football Federation, and they draw large, excited crowds when they play. Vietnam also has men's and women's national teams that compete in international competitions.

Martial arts, such as karate, judo, and kung fu, are also popular sports in Vietnam. In the 2000 Summer Olympics, Tran Hieu Ngan won a silver medal in women's tae kwon do, making her the first Vietnamese athlete to win an Olympic medal. Hoang Anh Tuan earned the country's second Olympic medal, also silver, in men's weight lifting in 2008.

Throughout the country, people participate in various sports. Large numbers of young people play soccer, and many other sports enthusiasts enjoy cycling, swimming, badminton, and tennis. Table tennis and volleyball are popular, too. Along the coast, people enjoy swimming, snorkeling, and scuba diving.

CHAPTER TEN

Daily Life

Millions of people live in Vietnam, and they all have their daily routines. People have their own way of doing things, their own habits, their own style. But one thing that they probably all have in common is that family is at the center of daily life.

Opposite: **One-quarter of the Vietnamese people are under age fifteen.**

Dining

It is common in Vietnam to eat out during the day, but the evening meal is usually shared with family at home. Across the country, it is easy to grab a quick breakfast and lunch. There are many street vendors selling tasty, inexpensive food, and cafés and restaurants are plentiful.

One common breakfast dish, especially in the northern part of the country, is *pho*, a noodle soup in a thick beef or chicken broth. Often the broth contains thin strips of meat. The dish is seasoned with ginger, fennel, roasted onion, or

Pho is a popular street food.

cinnamon. In the south, people eat *hu tieu*, which is similar to pho but includes vegetables. For lunch, many Vietnamese have a bowl of rice mixed with meat and vegetables.

Dinners commonly consist of seafood, salad, and fresh vegetables. Vietnamese do not typically end their meals with dessert, but sometimes they have fresh fruit.

The Flavor of Vietnam

Almost every recipe in Vietnam includes a fish sauce called *nuoc mam*. If a dish does not include this distinctive sauce, there is usually a bottle of it on every table so diners can add it themselves. It is a classic Vietnamese flavor.

At one time, nuoc mam was homemade, but now most Vietnamese buy it already prepared. To make nuoc mam, wooden barrels are filled with small, silver-colored fish, called *ca com*, packed between layers of salt. This mixture is left to sit for about three months. Then the juice that has gathered at the bottom of the barrel is removed and poured back over the top. After six more months, the juice is removed from the barrel again. This time it is ready to use. Sometimes it is bottled plain. Other times it is mixed with hot peppers, garlic, or lime juice.

From Birth to Death

Until recently, Vietnamese fathers were not present for the births of their children. Now, however, it is common for a father to take part. Usually visitors are not allowed to see the new baby for the first month because it is considered bad luck. When the baby is three months old, a naming ceremony is held. Babies are considered one year old when they are born. The Vietnamese do not celebrate the actual day they were born. Instead, they add another year to their age during Tet, the new year celebration.

Many Vietnamese carry their babies on their back.

In the past, Vietnamese parents arranged the marriages of their children. This does not often happen today, but it is still important for young Vietnamese to get their parents' approval before getting married. Women usually marry in their late teens or early twenties, while men typically marry between the ages of twenty and thirty. Most weddings take place in the family home. A Christian couple, however, usually marries in a church. During the ceremony, the bride and groom share small cups of wine with their families, pray, and exchange rings. Then the families gather for a reception. The newlyweds make the rounds to thank everyone for the gifts, which are typically money.

A couple has a traditional wedding in a temple in Ho Chi Minh City.

A funeral procession winds its way through the streets.

Funerals take place within a few days of someone's death. In keeping with Vietnamese tradition of worshipping deceased family members, an altar is put up in the family home and adorned with photos. During this time, Buddhist monks may offer prayers. Friends and extended family visit to share memories, express sympathy, and burn incense. After two days of mourning, the coffin is brought to the tomb in a funeral procession. Family members follow on foot.

Clothing

In cities, the clothes that most Vietnamese people wear is much like that worn by people in the United States and Canada. Fashionable western clothing is popular, especially among younger and wealthier people. But many Vietnamese still wear traditional clothing when dressing for special family

Many Vietnamese women wear the ao dai at celebrations and festivals. It is also a common school and work uniform.

occasions. For women and girls, this means an *ao dai*, a long dress with a slit up the side that is worn over a loose-fitting pair of slacks. The traditional formal outfit for men and boys is called an *ao the.* It is a long gown, usually brown or black, with a slit on the side. It is worn over pants.

National Holidays

New Year's Day	January 1
Tet	January or February
Hung Kings' Festival	April
Liberation Day	April 30
International Workers' Day	May 1
National Day	September 2

Mid-Autumn Festival

One of the most popular holidays in Vietnam is Tet Trung Thu, the Mid-Autumn Festival. Children are at the center of this festival. They carry lanterns in an early-morning procession. Some children put on large lion costumes and mimic a lion's movement in what is called the lion dance. People make and wear masks and tell folktales. And everyone enjoys eating mooncakes, pastries filled with seeds, sausages, coconut, or other delicious foods.

In rural areas, some people wear traditional clothing every day. They often wear hats to protect themselves from the sun. Many choose a traditional cone-shaped hat called a *non la.* These hats are made from woven palm leaves and are held in place with a string under the chin.

The non la offers excellent protection from the sun and rain.

Childhood Fun

Many Vietnamese children living in rural areas are expected to help their families tend to rice or other crops. But like children everywhere, when they have free time they enjoy playing games.

Playing with spinning tops is fun for many Vietnamese children. Those who do not have tops often carve their own or play using pieces of guava fruit. Vietnamese children also like to play with jacks made of bamboo, and they take part in many games involving running and catching.

Children and adults alike enjoy flying kites. The kites, which are often homemade, may be elaborate. Some have several layers of wings, and some even include small flutes that make music as the kites fly.

Students play in the sea after school.

Catch the Tail

Rong ran is a game played by large groups of children throughout Vietnam. One child is the doctor, while the others hang on to each other to form the long body of a dragon-snake. The game begins with the doctor questioning the dragon-snake, and the dragon-snake answering. Then the chase begins. The doctor tries to catch the tail of the dragon-snake, but the child who is the tail of the dragon-snake runs quickly to catch the head of the dragon-snake, forming a circle to keep the doctor out. If the doctor catches the tail before the circle can close, the children forming the dragon-snake lose the game. If they complete the circle, they win.

Past and Future

In recent decades, Vietnam has undergone tremendous changes. It had been a traditional society, where most people farmed and fished for what they needed. Then it was ravaged by war, its landscape devastated, and its people left with physical and emotional scars. At the war's end, the country became communist and closed off from much of the world.

When economic reforms opened Vietnam to the rest of the world, the nation changed rapidly. Today, many Vietnamese have the latest technology. Even rural areas have electricity and clean water. Supermarkets are taking the place of roadside vendors and traditional markets. In cities, motorbikes and cars are replacing the bicycle taxis that people used for transportation.

Some Vietnamese long for the old ways, while others are eager for modern conveniences. Vietnam is a country in flux, struggling to embrace what is new, while keeping the best of what is old.

A Vietnamese family takes a bicycle taxi across the Perfume River in Hue.

Timeline

Vietnamese History

The Dong Son culture is established.	1000 BCE
The Chinese conquer the northern part of what is now Vietnam; their cultural influence begins to spread.	111 BCE
The Trung sisters lead a successful revolt against the Chinese.	40 CE
Indian sailors establish ports on the southern coasts.	1st century CE
Chinese rule in Vietnam ends; Vietnam becomes an independent state.	938
The Ly dynasty begins.	1009
Vietnam's first university is established in Hanoi.	1076
The Tran dynasty begins.	1225
China regains control of Vietnam.	1407
Le Loi leads a successful revolt against China and establishes the Le dynasty.	1427
The Tay Son Rebellion occurs.	1788
Nguyen Anh unites the north and south regions and names the country Vietnam.	1802
France takes control of Vietnam.	1858

World History

ca. 2500 BCE	The Egyptians build the pyramids and the Sphinx in Giza.
ca. 563 BCE	The Buddha is born in India.
313 CE	The Roman emperor Constantine legalizes Christianity.
610	The Prophet Muhammad begins preaching a new religion called Islam.
1054	The Eastern (Orthodox) and Western (Roman Catholic) Churches break apart.
1095	The Crusades begin.
1215	King John seals the Magna Carta.
1300s	The Renaissance begins in Italy.
1347	The plague sweeps through Europe.
1453	Ottoman Turks capture Constantinople, conquering the Byzantine Empire.
1492	Columbus arrives in North America.
1500s	Reformers break away from the Catholic Church, and Protestantism is born.
1776	The U.S. Declaration of Independence is signed.
1789	The French Revolution begins.
1865	The American Civil War ends.

Vietnamese History

Ho Chi Minh founds the Indochinese Communist Party.	1930
Japan controls Vietnam.	1940–1945
The Viet Minh nationalist organization begins fighting for Vietnam's freedom.	1941
Vietnamese independence is declared.	1945
France resumes fighting for control of Vietnam.	1946
Vietnam is divided into North Vietnam and South Vietnam.	1954
The National Liberation Front forms in South Vietnam.	1960
President Ngo Dinh Diem of South Vietnam is assassinated.	1963
The United States begins bombing North Vietnam.	1964
North Vietnam launches the Tet Offensive against South Vietnam.	1968
The United States military pulls out of Vietnam.	1973
South Vietnam surrenders to North Vietnam.	1975
The Socialist Republic of Vietnam is created.	1976
The doi moi economic reforms begin.	1986
Vietnam and the United States establish full diplomatic relations.	1995
U.S. president Bill Clinton visits Vietnam.	2000
Truong Tan Sang is elected president.	2011

World History

1879	The first practical lightbulb is invented.
1914	World War I begins.
1917	The Bolshevik Revolution brings communism to Russia.
1929	A worldwide economic depression begins.
1939	World War II begins.
1945	World War II ends.
1969	Humans land on the Moon.
1975	The Vietnam War ends.
1989	The Berlin Wall is torn down as communism crumbles in Eastern Europe.
1991	The Soviet Union breaks into separate states.
2001	Terrorists attack the World Trade Center in New York City and the Pentagon near Washington, D.C.
2004	A tsunami in the Indian Ocean destroys coastlines in Africa, India, and Southeast Asia.
2008	The United States elects its first African American president.

Fast Facts

Official name: Socialist Republic of Vietnam
Capital: Hanoi
Official language: Vietnamese

Hanoi

National flag

Fan Si Pan

Official religion:	None
Year of founding:	1976
National anthem:	"Tien Quan Ca" ("Song of the Marching Army")
Type of government:	Communist state
Head of state:	President
Head of government:	Prime minister
Area of country:	127,882 square miles (331,212 sq km)
Latitude and longitude of geographic center:	16° N, 106° E
Bordering countries:	China is to the north; Laos and Cambodia are to the west
Highest elevation:	Fan Si Pan, 10,312 feet (3,143 m) above sea level
Lowest elevation:	Sea level, along the coast
Average high temperature:	Ho Chi Minh City: 89°F (32°C) in January; 90°F (32°C) in July. Hanoi: 67°F (19°C) in January; 91°F (33°C) in July
Average low temperature:	Ho Chi Minh City: 70°F (21°C) in January; 76°F (24°C) in July. Hanoi: 57°F (14°C) in January; 79°F (26°C) in July
Average annual precipitation:	78 inches (198 cm) in the Mekong Delta; 66 inches (168 cm) in the Red River delta

My Son Sanctuary

National population (2011 est.): 91,519,289

Population of major cities (2009 est.):

Ho Chi Minh City	7,396,446
Hanoi	6,472,200
Haiphong	1,907,705
Can Tho	1,187,089
Da Nang	887,069

Landmarks:

- ***Cat Ba National Park***, Haiphong
- ***Cu Chi Tunnels***, near Ho Chi Minh City
- ***Ha Long Bay***, Haiphong
- ***Marble Mountains***, Da Nang
- ***My Son Sanctuary***, Da Nang
- ***Thang Long Water Puppet Theater***, Hanoi

Currency

Economy: Industry is the main force in Vietnam's economy, making up about 41 percent of the country's overall income and employing about 20 percent of the workforce. Mining is a key industry, and coal is a major export. Phosphate, iron, tin, and chromium are also mined. Food processing is an important industry. Rice is the main crop in Vietnam, but peanuts, corn, sugarcane, cassava, and sweet potatoes are also important. Many Vietnamese make their living through fishing. Tourism and banking are growing industries.

Currency: The dong. In 2012, US$1.00 was equal to 21,000 dong.

System of weights and measures: Metric system

Literacy rate: 94%

Schoolchildren

Le Cong Vinh

Common Vietnamese words and phrases:

chào ban	hello, good-bye
Ban khóc không?	How are you?
lám on	please
cám on	thank you
Bà tên là gì?	What's your name?
Tôi tên là . . .	My name is . . .

Prominent Vietnamese:

Ho Chi Minh (1890–1969)
Military leader and president of North Vietnam

Le Cong Vinh (1985–)
Soccer player

Le Loi (ca. 1385–1433)
Founder of the Le dynasty

Ngo Dinh Diem (1901–1963)
First president of South Vietnam

Nguyen Du (1765–1820)
Poet

Trung Trac and Trung Nhi (?–43 CE)
Political leaders

To Find Out More

Books

- Gifford, Clive. *Why Did the Vietnam War Happen?* New York: Gareth Stevens, 2011.
- Lâm, Truong Búu. *A Story of Vietnam*. Parker, CO: Outskirts Press, 2010.
- Phillips, Douglas A. *Vietnam*. New York: Chelsea House Publications, 2006.
- Sterling, Richard. *Vietnam & Angkor Wat*. New York: DK Publishing, 2011.

Music

- Perfume River Ensemble. *Music from the Lost Kingdom: Hue Vietnam*. New York: Lyrichord Discs, 1998.
- *Rough Guide to the Music of Vietnam*. London: World Music Network, 2007.

▶ **Visit this Scholastic Web site for more information on Vietnam:**
www.factsfornow.scholastic.com
Enter the keyword Vietnam

Index

Page numbers in *italics* indicate illustrations.

Meet the Author

When Terri Willis was in the third grade, her brother, Tom, was a soldier fighting in the Vietnam War. That connection gave her a greater interest in Vietnam than most of her peers had. She read his letters, watched the evening news, and listened intently to adult conversations about the war. Still, her impression of Vietnam was limited to the things a little girl could understand: it was steamy hot; there was jungle; there were mountains; the bugs were big.

As she grew older, Willis held on to her interest in Vietnam, even after her brother arrived home safely. She tried to fill in the blanks that she had missed as a youngster. While she was correct, at least in part, about the climate, terrain, and insect life, there was definitely much more for her to learn about the Vietnamese people, their culture and history, and the reasons the U.S. military became involved in the region. The research that she did for this book expanded on the research she has done throughout her life as she has tried to gain a greater understanding of Vietnam and correct her earlier assumptions. She says she is fortunate to have the opportunity to share some of that information with a new generation of young people through this book.

Willis is a graduate of the University of Wisconsin–Madison, with a degree in journalism. She has edited and written books for young people for twenty years, focusing on geographic, historic, and environmental topics. The titles that she has written for Scholastic's Enchantment of the World series include *Afghanistan*, *Libya*, *The Democratic Republic of the Congo*, *Lebanon*, and *Venezuela*.

Willis and her husband, Harold, have two daughters who are in college. They make their home in Cedarburg, Wisconsin, where she also works as a substitute teacher, mainly for middle school students, her favorite age group. "Any time I'm having difficulty writing about a topic," says Willis, "I imagine myself in front of my favorite students and think about how I would explain it to them. I try to address the things they might find curious and answer the questions they might ask."

Photo Credits

Photographs © 2013:

age fotostock: 11 (Aldo Pavan), 116 (Chederros), 94 (Christophe Boisvieux), 8 (Didier Forray), 125 top (Dr Mart Baumgärtner), 15, 131 bottom (FLPA/Keith Rushforth), 72, 114 (Ingolf Pompe), 80 (M Yousuf Tushar), 113 left (Rene Mattes), back cover (Stu Smucker);

Alamy Images: 44 (Cyril Hou), 74 (dave stamboulis), 90 (David R. Frazier Photolibrary, Inc.), 29 (Olga Khoroshunova), 24 (Paul Rushton), 39 (Peter Horree), 7 bottom, 34 (Terry Whittaker);

AP Images: 62 right (AH), 22 (Alberto Marquez), 117, 133 bottom (Chitose Suzuki), 61 (Eddie Adams), 20 top (Eugene Hoshiko), 58 (Frank Waters), 126 (Julien Behal), 66 (Kim Lien), 25 (VNA), 54 top, 56;

Art Resource/Erich Lessing/Musee des Arts Asiatiques-Guimet, Paris, France: 36;

Dreamstime/Tudor Antonel Adrian: 68, 131 top;

Getty Images: 78 bottom (CNES/CSG/AFP), 18, 65 (Hoang Dinh Nam/AFP), 121 (John W Banagan), 2 (Kimberley Coole), 12 (Martin Puddy), 92, 127 (Peter Stuckings), 85 (Stu Smucker);

iStockphoto: 125 bottom (lubilub), 54 bottom (Zhan Tian);

Landov: 70 (EPA/STR), 73 (Kham/Reuters);

Media Bakery: 31 (Deddeda), 33 (Gerhard Zwerger-Schoner);

Newscom: 102 (Craig Lovell Stock Connection USA), 120 bottom (Hoang Dinh Nam/AFP/Getty Images);

Photo Researchers/Terry Whittaker: 35;

Shutterstock, Inc.: 50 (Antonio Abrignani), 19 bottom (kowit sitthi), 20 bottom (Luciano Mortula), 81, 132 bottom (Miroslav Hladik), 120 top (Quang Ho), 30 (Stacy Funderburke), 87 (Stephen Bures);

Superstock, Inc.: 19 top, 21, 99 (age fotostock), 122, 123 (Asia Images), 16 (Axiom Photographic Limited), 40 (Bridgeman Art Library, London), 76 (Dave Stamboulis/age fotostock), 38 (DeAgostini), 82, 130 left (Gonzalo Azumendi/age fotostock), 89, 100, 105, 118, 133 top (imagebroker.net), 115 (LatitudeStock), 23, 111 (Le-Dung Ly/Science Faction), 7 top, 17, 28, 104 (Lonely Planet), 91 (Melba/age fotostock), 113 right (Melvin Longhurst), 62 left, 101, 103, 106, 108 (Photononstop), 59 (Prisma), 41, 43 top, 46, 69 top, 95 right, 107, 132 top (Robert Harding Picture Library), 42, 47, 88 right (Steve Vidler), cover, 6 (Tibor Bognár/age fotostock), 26 (Tier und Naturfotografie), 43 bottom (Travel Pix Collection/Jon Arnold Images), 97 (Universal Images Group);

The Image Works: 96 (Alain Evrard/Impact/HIP), 51 (Alinari Archives), 112 (Bruno Pérousse/akg-images), 48, 77, 88 left, 95 left (David R. Frazier), 63 (Françoise Demulder/Roger-Viollet), 110 (Jak Kilby/ArenaPal), 98 (Kristina Eriksson/Sueddeutsche Zeitung Photo), 52 (RIA Novosti), 55 (Roger-Viollet), 69 bottom right (Sean Sprague), 60 (TopFoto), 53 (Weltbild/ullstein bild), 32 (World History Archive/Topfoto);

Thinkstock/iStockphoto: 124.

Maps by XNR Productions, Inc.